LEVI ROOTS'
REGGAE REGGAE
COOKBOOK

LEVI ROOTS'

REGGAE REGGAE

PUT SOME MUSIC IN YOUR FOOD WITH THESE 80 DELICIOUS CARIBBEAN-INSPIRED RECIPES

COOKBOOK

HarperCollins*Publishers*

For my grandmother and my mother

WHEN USING KITCHEN APPLIANCES PLEASE ALWAYS
FOLLOW THE MANUFACTURER'S INSTRUCTIONS

HarperCollins*Publishers*
1 London Bridge Street
London SE1 9GF
www.harpercollins.co.uk

HarperCollins*Publishers*
Macken House, 39/40 Mayor Street Upper
Dublin 1, D01 C9W8, Ireland

First published by HarperCollins*Publishers* 2008
This edition published 2025

10 9 8 7 6 5 4 3 2 1

Text © Levi Roots 2008, 2025
Photography © David Munns 2008 (except
those listed on page 192)
Illustrations © Peter Webb, 2008

Levi Roots asserts the moral right to be
identified as the author of this work

A catalogue record of this book is
available from the British Library

ISBN 978-0-00-870988-4

Photographer: David Munns
Food Stylist: Felicity Barnum-Bobb

Printed and bound by GPS

MIX
Paper | Supporting
responsible forestry
FSC™ C007454

This book is produced from FSC™ certified paper and other
controlled sources to ensure responsible forest management.

For more information visit:
www.harpercollins.co.uk/green

CONTENTS

FOREWORD BY
PETER JONES

I have been asked to write this foreword for a man who
in less than one year went from budding entrepreneur
to household name – a man who goes by the name of
Levi Roots. Well, that's what he said his name was when
he appeared in front of me on the TV show 'Dragons' Den'.
It was only after a few questions that Levi revealed that his
real name was Keith Graham. I thought he'd got the wrong
studio and had arrived to take part in some kind of audition
for a music show! No-one had ever come into the Den before
with a guitar and dreadlocks and so much confidence.
Anything less like a stereotypical 'businessman' would be
hard to imagine. But it wasn't just his name that got my
attention and it wasn't just his pitch, the way he looked
or his product, it was all of those things and more.

That day was the day I met a great man with a dream.
A year and a bit on, after choosing to back this incredible
man, I remember the hours, days, perhaps even weeks
both my team and I have spent working with him as
some of the most enjoyable and exciting times of 2007.

Anyone wanting to start out on that long road to business
success would be better for knowing Levi's inspiring and
passionate journey. Dreams can become reality with the
right mindset. One of the reasons for Levi's popularity and

for his success is his passion for life, unbounding energy and enthusiasm for everything he does. He has a 'keep on keeping on' attitude which has meant that despite all of the challenges he has faced, which he discusses in this book, he has never given up.

I am positive you are going to enjoy reading this book. It will bring you even closer to a man I have been pleased to help and who I am even more pleased to call my friend. Levi Roots has firmly established himself as the face of Caribbean food in the UK, a dream that he has nurtured throughout his whole life. I've often said that business is the new rock n' roll, and if so then Levi Roots is Elvis Presley!

But this book is not about business. It's an education in the fun, flavour, music and vibrancy of a Caribbean culture that we in the UK don't know that much about. I certainly hadn't tried jerk chicken, until my first Reggae Reggae experience, and now I'm hooked! I hope you enjoy relaxing, trying out the recipes with your friends and family, and putting some music in your food! Dreams do certainly come true and Levi, it has been an honour to be part of yours.

INTRODUCTION

My culinary journey has been nothing short of incredible. Every time I close my eyes, it seems as if it was only yesterday that I was selling a few bottles of my homemade Jerk sauce, which was inspired by my grandmother, to local people at Brixton Market in southwest London. Then when I open my eyes, I always marvel at seeing and knowing that my Reggae Reggae Sauce is now available in almost every major supermarket around the UK. And for that, I'd like to say a huge thank you to everyone who has supported this and all my other products over the years.

With this book, you will be getting the very best of me. I suppose that is why it is my only book that carries the title so associated with my most famous product, the one that marks my victory in BBC TV's Dragons' Den programme, when I absolutely slayed those Dragons with my business pitch and walked away with £50,000 and two influential business investors as mentors and partners.

You see, my love for cooking, mixing and blending Caribbean herbs and spices has always been my driving force, and I cannot think of anything more satisfying and inspirational than bashing together fragrant fresh thyme, aromatic allspice berries, zesty lime, juicy garlic and, of course, fiery Scotch bonnet chillies with my pestle and mortar, then inhaling all the fabulous aromas that are released.

My other key ingredient in my recipes is my love for music – reggae music in particular. In some ways, for me, cooking is a bit like composing my very own symphonies in a saucepan, combining all the flavours, experiencing the amazing smells, the tastes, the excitement, the expectation and the anticipation of what is to come. To me, this is always divine. Dancing around in the kitchen with the sound of reggae music blasting away is not uncommon for me – especially when I've got a barbecue on the go. That's when all my best moves come out!

I have found that one of the best things to bring people together is food, particularly Caribbean cuisine, where the flavours are spicy, wild and strong. Caribbean cuisine demands that you start with a happy and excited vibe because that is how you will get the best out of yourself and the fantastic ingredients used in the recipes. And I'm not just talking about the strong Jamaican rum that might be on offer, but music, laughter, fun and party vibes. All of these are part of that mixture that will give your home-cooked Caribbean food Levi Roots styleee.

I am truly hoping that you will place this book somewhere that's easily within reach, so you can have as much fun in the kitchen as I do. I have crammed almost all the iconic Jamaican foods into the chapters here for you, including Ackee and Saltfish (the national dish), as well as an amazing slow-cooked curried goat recipe, which is everyone's favourite choice from Caribbean takeaways, but now you can cook it yourself!

It wouldn't be a Reggae Reggae recipe book without my Jerk Chicken and Rice and Peas, which are now legendary. There's a recipe for Fried Plantain too, and an Oxtail and Butter Bean Stew that's to die for. I've also included popular street food like Jamaican patties and festivals and fritters. Vegetarians – I've got you covered: check out my Hot Ital Stew, Ital Red Pea Soup, Rasta Pasta and lots more. Drinks are also in abundance, including my fave Guinness Punch, and there are some amazing cakes, bakes and dessert for anyone with a sweet tooth.

So get in that kitchen or around that BBQ, put on your favourite music and infuse your food with some music.

More love,

LR

CARIBBEAN INGREDIENTS AND TERMS

Lots of the ingredients in this book are readily available in the supermarkets. For the more unusual ones, check out your local ethnic shops and you'll probably find more of them than you'd think.

ACKEE

Before it's fully ripe, ackee looks like a large pink mango and is poisonous to eat. When ripe, it bursts open into a 'smile', revealing yellow flesh with black seeds. It is most widely available canned, although it can be slightly expensive. It has a lovely silky texture which some people compare to that of scrambled eggs.

ALL-PURPOSE SEASONING

Caribbean food relies heavily on seasoning and this is a commercially prepared blend of spices. The ingredients in different brands vary; they include salt, paprika, chilli powder, celery powder, ground coriander, onion powder and can also include allspice, garlic, thyme and black pepper. Make sure the brand you use doesn't contain MSG (monosodium glutamate).

ALLSPICE

Allspice berries, also called pimento seeds, are the dried berries from a pimento tree. Their distinctive flavour, similar to a mixture of cloves, cinnamon and nutmeg, is a vital ingredient in jerk seasoning. If using whole berries, use them to cook and flavour the dish but remove before eating (as you would cloves). Allspice is also available ground.

BANANAS

The most well known variety is obviously the sweet yellow banana. There is also the PLANTAIN, a savoury variety which is much larger and chunkier and best enjoyed when the yellow skin is beginning to blacken. They cannot be eaten raw, so must be fried, boiled or baked. GREEN BANANAS are smaller and must also be cooked before eating.

BEANS

When Caribbeans talk about 'peas', they actually mean beans, and not the green pea as we know it. So the Jamaican favourite, 'rice and peas', is actually rice with red kidney beans. Beans are a Caribbean staple, used in soups, stews and side dishes. Traditionally, they were used fresh, but these days they are most commonly available dried. Dried beans require soaking overnight before use. Then boil vigorously for 10 minutes to kill off their poisonous toxins and simmer until tender. You can buy canned beans, but unfortunately these don't produce the flavoursome pink liquid which comes from the boiling process. Favourite varieties include kidney beans, black beans, gunga peas (also called pigeon peas) and black eyed peas (also called cowpeas).

BREADFRUIT

This is a large cannonball-sized starchy vegetable that can be used either when green or when ripe. Treat it as you would potatoes; try it thinly sliced and fried, cubed and roasted in the oven with oil, barbecued whole or even boiled and mashed with butter.

BROWN

Jamaican dishes are often called 'brown' or 'brown-down' – this simply refers to the fish or meat being browned in a little oil before any liquid is added.

CALLALOO

Popular in soups and stews, callaloo is an exotic alternative to spinach. The name is used for the green leaves from a wide variety of plants, including taro (also called dasheen),

Plantain
Green Bananas

Breadfruit

Callaloo
CALLALOO

Christophene

tannia (also called malnga) and amaranth (prickly callaloo). The leaves need to be washed, chopped and boiled in the same way as spinach. Callaloo is available canned, but if you can't find it try using large spinach leaves as a substitute.

CHRISTOPHENE

In Jamaica, this is also known as 'cho-cho' or 'chayote'. It is a pear-shaped gourd with a delicate flavour, similar in taste and texture to a young squash, or small marrow. The most commonly available variety is pale green and the skin can be either prickly or smooth. Peel before using and try it raw in salads, or boiled in soups or stews.

CINNAMON

Cinnamon sticks are rolled up quills of the dried pale-brown inner bark of the cinnamon tree. Cinnamon trees grow naturally on many of the Caribbean islands, notably Grenada. In Barbados, cinnamon is simply called 'spice' because it's used so much. As well as quills, it may be sold as strips of bark (sometimes known as cinnamon leaf) or as a ground powder. It's a key ingredient in jerk seasoning.

COCO BREAD

This is a firm, white, slightly sweet bread, traditional in Jamaica, and often a part of Caribbean takeaways. It is called coco bread because you split it open like a coconut. Similar to a pitta, it makes an ideal pocket for other ingredients and is traditionally eaten filled with a vegetable patty. As an alternative, you'll find hard dough bread in large supermarkets and West Indian bakers. Bagels would also make a good substitute.

COCONUT

Green coconuts, called Jelly coconuts, are readily available in the Caribbean. They have a green shell and a jelly-like interior. They are very tough to open, so you will need a strong kitchen knife or meat cleaver to slice off the top or pierce a hole. Inside you'll find the coconut water, which you can drink with a straw – be careful not to spill it, though, because it stains!

Brown coconuts, (or dry coconuts) are more widely available in the UK and contain coconut water and coconut flesh. The flesh can be grated and mixed with water to make coconut milk.

Coconut milk is the liquid from the coconut, mixed with grated coconut meat. This can be bought in cans.

Coconut cream is thicker, with a greater density of coconut and less water.

Creamed coconut is compressed coconut flesh, with no water and is sold as a solid block. Crumble or grate it into liquids to add the flavour.

Desiccated coconut is dried grated coconut. It is often used in sweet cakes and breads.

Sweetened tenderised coconut is desiccated coconut that has a softer texture, since it has been sweetened with sugar. This is also a great ingredient for sweet cakes and breads.

Coconuts

Mixed Essence

Browning

Okra

Yam

Sweet Potatoes

CORNMEAL

Cornmeal is a yellow grain, ground from corn (maize). The name varies across the Caribbean from island to island and it is also commonly referred to using the Italian name, polenta. It's used in savoury and sweet dishes, including cornmeal dumplings and a pudding called cornmeal pone.

DUCHY

'Duchy' is an abbreviation of the traditional Dutch pot used for cooking many Caribbean dishes, including roasts, stews and soups. Made of aluminium and originally used to cook over an open fire, a duchy holds a lot of heat in its sides and lid, so food cooks quickly and thoroughly. Remember the old song lyrics ' pass the duchy pan the left hand side'?

ESCOVITCH

Like 'ceviche', its European equivalent, this refers to food that is cooked with vinegar.

GRAVY BROWNING

This is a ready-made liquid available in large supermarkets. It's a great time-saver and gives certain dishes, such as stewed beef or oxtail, a good strong brown colour. If not available, see the recipe for Brown Down Chicken (see page 50), for an alternative method of browning.

JERK AND JERK SEASONING

Jerk is the traditional Jamaican way to cook pork, chicken, beef and seafood over a fire pit or on a closed barbeque smoke pit. It was brought to the island over 250 years ago with the African slaves. Nowadays Jamaicans use an oil drum cut in half and used as you would a lidded barbecue.

Jamaican jerk seasoning is a traditional marinade used to spice up chicken, meat and fish, usually before barbequing. It can be bought ready prepared or you can make your own (see page 131 for my recipe). Jerk generally contains spring onion, bell chilli peppers, salt, thyme, allspice and cinnamon.

MIXED CARIBBEAN ESSENCE

This is a commercially prepared product that combines the flavours of vanilla, almond and lemon. If not available, make your own by mixing equal quantities of vanilla essence, almond essence and lemon juice.

OKRA

These are also called ladies fingers, presumably because they look like elegant pointy green digits! A relative of the cotton plant, this vegetable has the mild flavour of a runner-bean but is one of the least liked vegetables in the West, because of its slimy texture. However, it features lots in Caribbean recipes, and very successfully too! Its natural thickening qualities are ideal for sauces and soups. It's also great steamed as a vegetable and enjoyed with fish, or blanched in a salad. Choose small pods, and keep them whole; the more you slice them, the slimier the finished dish!

POTATOES

Regular potatoes are often called 'Irish Potata' by Caribbean cooks. Sweet potatoes can be treated just as you would regular potatoes. Their skin varies in colour from brown to purple and the flesh can be either white or orange. In the USA they are known as sweet yams.

SALTFISH

Also called codfish or salted cod, this recipe was a way of preserving fish in the hot Caribbean climate. The fish is dried and then heavily salted. Before use, it needs to be rinsed, or soaked in water, then boiled a couple of times to remove excess saltiness. Often sold in a block, this contains bones, which need to be removed after boiling but before frying. Salt fish fillets are easier to use but more expensive.

SCOTCH BONNET CHILLI PEPPERS

Hot peppers give Caribbean food its distinctive flavour. Sometimes called bird pepper, country pepper or seasoning pepper, the scotch bonnet pepper is the most favoured in Jamaica. So-called because its irregular sides resemble a bonnet, it is available in a variety of colours from yellow and green through to red and is only about an inch long. It is extremely hot with a slightly bitter flavour (the heat comes from the seeds, so remove if you prefer a milder dish). If not available, use chilli peppers instead or add a splash of West Indian Hot Pepper sauce for a more authentic taste.

YAM

This is a starchy root vegetable available in many different types, varying in size, shape and colour. The most common are those with yellow and white flesh. The bark-like skin may be smooth or rough, pale in colour, brown or purple. They have quite a bland starchy flavour, but treat them as you would potatoes and try them boiled, mashed, fried or roasted.

Scotch Bonnet Chillies

REGGAE ESSENTIALS

Get started with these easy Caribbean classics and simple side dishes.

Levi's Rice

Rinse the rice several times (this removes the starch), draining off the excess water.

Bring a large pan of water to the boil, add salt to taste, make sure it's boiling and add the butter.

Add the rice ensuring that the top of the water is no more than a fork's tine above the water. Drain off the excess water if needed. Stir, bring back to the boil, then cover and simmer for 20 minutes. Don't be tempted to lift the lid!

Leave the rice to cool for 5 minutes, then fluff up and serve.

Serves 4

600g/1lb 5oz basmati rice
salt
knob of butter

ROOTS RECOMMENDS:
The water should be no more than
2.5cm/1in above the rice in the pan. If it
is more then drain or ladle off the excess.

Boiled Provisions

Cook up a mix of filling and slightly sweet vegetables for a traditional Jamaican change to rice or potatoes. They go very well with meats and stews.

Put the yam, sweet potatoes, green bananas and plantain into a large saucepan of salted water Bring to the boil, then reduce the heat and simmer for 25 minutes until the vegetables are just soft – check by pushing in a fork.

Drain, then peel the bananas and cut into 2 pieces. Peel the plantain and cut into 4 pieces and serve the vegetables topped with the butter.

Serves 4

350g/12oz piece yam, peeled and cut into 4 pieces
350g/12oz sweet potatoes, peeled and cut into 4 pieces
2 green bananas, topped, tailed and skin removed
1 ripe plantain, topped, tailed and slit down 1 side
salt
knob of butter

Boiled and Fried Breadfruit

To cook the breadfruit, bring a large pan of salted water to the boil. Add the breadfruit and boil for 15 minutes until it is almost tender. Drain.

Cut each wedge into 3 pieces to make slices.

Heat the oil in a large frying pan, add the breadfruit slices and fry for a few minutes on each side until golden. Remove and drain on kitchen paper to get rid of the excess oil. Sprinkle with parsley and serve.

Serves 4

½ breadfruit, peeled and cut into 4 large wedges

salt

3 tbsp vegetable oil, for frying

1 tbsp fresh flat-leaf parsley, chopped

Boiled Green Bananas

Green bananas aren't regular bananas that haven't ripened – they're totally different!

Cut the tops and tails off the green bananas and cut a slit down one side. Peel away the skin.

Bring a large saucepan of salted water to the boil and add the green bananas. Bring back to the boil, then reduce the heat and simmer for about 20 minutes or until the bananas are tender.

Using a slotted spoon, remove the bananas from the pan and leave until cool enough to handle. Peel away the skin and cut each one into 2–3 chunks.

Serves 4

4 green bananas

salt

Rice and Peas

Peas are what most Jamaicans call red kidney beans. This is one of our most important dishes and we serve it with many different things. It has a subtle coconut flavour that goes well with many dishes. The crucial thing here is to get the perfect proportion of rice and liquid to make free-flowing tender rice.

Serves 4

175g/6oz dried red kidney beans

1 whole coconut or 200g/7oz block creamed coconut, grated

3–4 tsp salt

knob of butter

1 whole Scotch bonnet chilli

1 spring onion, green end only, chopped

1 fresh thyme sprig

1 garlic clove

1 tsp all-purpose seasoning

500g/1lb 2oz pure basmati rice

Rinse the beans in cold water, then put them in a large bowl and cover with 1 litre/1¾ pints cold water. Leave to soak overnight.

Don't throw the soaking water away! Drain the soaking water into a large pan and bring it to the boil.

Meanwhile, rinse the beans under cold running water and throw any damaged ones away. Add the beans to the boiling water, bring back to the boil, cover and boil vigorously for 10 minutes (you have to do this to get rid of the poisonous toxins). Reduce the heat and simmer for a further 35 minutes until the beans are really soft. To test, squeeze them.

Smash the coconut on the floor (mind your toes), crack open and drain off the coconut liquid, reserving the liquid. Remove the 'meat' from the shell carefully with a sharp knife and grate into a bowl. Add the reserved coconut liquid, then pour in 1 litre/1¾ pints hot water and stir well. If you are using the creamed coconut, mix with 2 litres/3½ pints hot water.

Add the coconut, salt, butter, chilli, spring onion, thyme, garlic and all-purpose seasoning to the pan of beans and boil for 15–20 minutes.

Now, rinse the rice twice under cold running water, drain, then add to the pan. Make sure the liquid is 2.5/1in above the level of the rice. Cook for 20–25 minutes on a really gentle heat until all the water is absorbed and the rice is tender. DO NOT LIFT THE LID during cooking because you'll release all the moisture. When the rice is cooked, put clingfilm or foil over the top to seal and cover.

ROOTS RECOMMENDS:
Basically, you need just over double the amount of liquid to rice. Once the rice is in the pan, never add water because the rice will go cloggy and horrible.

Fried Plantain

Choose a ripe plantain with black pigmentation and make sure it is flexible. Plantain that are unripe are starchy, hard and not sweet.

Cut the plantain in half, then cut off the ends so you check that the plantain is undamaged. Cut a slit down the groove on each piece of plantain and peel off the skin. Slice thickly.

Heat the oil in a frying pan until it's fairly hot, add the plantain, reduce the heat and cook gently for 2–3 minutes on each side until golden brown. Serve.

Serves 3 as a side dish

1 large plantain
4 tbsp vegetable oil

Fried Dumplings

Put the flour and salt into a large bowl, add the butter. Use your hands, rub it in until the mixture forms crumbs. Gradually add most of 250ml/9fl oz water until the mixture comes together to form a ball.

Using your hands, knead the mixture for a few minutes. If the dough is too dry, add a little more water, then continue to knead until a soft dough forms and the bowl is clean.

Heat the oil in a large, deep frying pan.

Divide the dough into 12 pieces. Take each piece of dough and knead until it is stretchy, then roll each one into a smooth ball.

Check to see if the oil is hot enough by taking a tiny piece of the dough and dropping it into the hot oil. If it is just bubbling around the edges, it's ready.

Meanwhile, shape each ball into a flat cake. Gradually add them in batches to the pan of hot oil. Keep the temperature really low while you fry them. Cook for about 5 minutes, then carefully turn them over when the underside is pale golden and they are starting to look puffy. Fry for a further 5 minutes until they are golden and cooked through. Drain on kitchen paper and serve.

Makes 12

400g/14oz self-raising flour
1 tsp salt
50g/2oz butter, cut into cubes
400ml/14fl oz vegetable oil

Festival

These are the Caribbean rivals to doughnuts. They're quick to make as they are yeast free. They are a wicked breakfast treat on their own, but you can also serve them with food such as steamed fish

Heat the oil in a large deep frying pan. Put the flour, cornmeal, baking powder, salt, cinnamon, nutmeg, sugar and butter into a large bowl and, using your hands, rub the butter into the flour mixture until the mixture forms fine crumbs.

Now take it easy – in Jamaica we always used to say 'you're not a good cook if you spoil the flour', so just add 100ml/3½fl oz water to make a smooth dough and knead it all together. If you think the mixture is a little wet, sprinkle with some flour – you don't want the dough to be at all sticky.

Take small pieces of the dough and roll them into sausage shapes, then flatten each one with the side of your hand.

Check to see if the oil is hot enough, then deep-fry the festivals for a couple of minutes on one side until they are golden. Turn them over very carefully, because they are delicate and fry for another couple of minutes until completely brown. Drain and serve.

Makes 6

600ml/1 pint vegetable oil, for deep frying

175g/6oz plain flour

50g/2oz fine cornmeal

1 tsp baking powder

1 tsp salt

1 tsp ground cinnamon

¼ tsp freshly ground nutmeg

75g/3oz soft brown or demerara sugar

25g/1oz butter

'What no good fe breakfast,
no good fe dinnah'

Season Rice

Seasoning meat and fish in Caribbean food is the vital step that separates it from European food. Caribbean cooking usually calls for more seasoning than just salt and pepper to give it a gorgeous spicy flavour. The longer you leave the food to season the better it will taste because all the spices and flavourings will have soaked right through the centre and, boy, you'll be begging for more.

Rinse the salt cod in warm water to dissolve the salt, then put into a pan and cover with warm water. Bring to the boil and boil for 5 minutes. Drain and rinse again. Break up the fish into small pieces.

Bring 1 litre/1¾ pints cold water to the boil in a large pan, add the pumpkin, spring onion, onion, peppers, thyme and salt cod. Bring back to the boil and cook for 10 minutes until the pumpkin has softened.

Now rinse the rice twice under cold running water and drain (this takes the starch away). Add the rice to the pan with the butter and peas and stir well. Make sure the water is at least 2.5cm/1in above the level of the rice. Ladle away any surplus. Bring to the boil, cover, then reduce the heat to the lowest possible setting and simmer for about 15 minutes or until the rice is tender and the liquid is absorbed. Do not uncover during cooking.

Use a fork to mix everything evenly together and to separate the rice grains before serving.

Serves 4

175g/6oz skinless, boneless salt cod

300g/10oz pumpkin, peeled and grated

1 spring onion, green end only, finely chopped

½ onion, chopped

¼ green pepper, deseeded and chopped

¼ red pepper, deseeded and chopped

1 fresh thyme sprig, chopped

700g/1lb 9oz basmati rice

knob of butter

a handful of frozen peas (about 50g/2oz)

MY LIFE IN JAMAICA

I was born in 1958 in a little Jamaican village called Content, the youngest of six children. Content could not have been better named. It was a tiny country village, and my memories of it are of sunshine, freedom, great food and being happy. It was exactly how a childhood should be.

My real name is Keith Valentine Graham, but nobody in Content called me that. Everybody called me Willesley. I still have no idea why. It was just my pet name: a lot of people in Jamaica have them. It's an old English name, and even now I occasionally see roads that are called that in London.

In the early 1960s, the British government started telling people in the West Indies, 'Come to England, the streets are paved with gold!' Everybody believed it; but then of course when they got to England and found that they weren't paved with gold, they were covered in dog mess, and we were the ones who were expected to clean it up!

So, when I was four my parents emigrated to England to try to make a better life for us. Like all Jamaican parents, they wanted their kids to be doctors, or lawyers, and they had to leave Content to have any chance of making that happen.

My father, Lascell Vincent, left for London first and my mother, Doreen May, followed a few months later. I will never forget the day she left. She told me she was leaving and not coming back but I was so young it seemed like she was just going to the market, or down the road to Kingston. But I can remember waving goodbye to her and chasing after the car as she left for the airport.

My parents moved to Brixton in south London and left us kids with my wonderful grandparents. My parents worked and saved and every year they sent for another of the kids; the eldest first, then the next eldest, and so on. So every year I waved goodbye to another one of my siblings.

In Jamaica, we all shared two rooms in my grandmother's house, so the only good thing about the departures was that every year we could stretch out a little more! It seemed an unthinkable luxury to have your own room, like I knew my brothers and sisters had in London.

My grandmother was so special. She always fussed over me because I was the youngest. She was very beautiful – dark and slim, with long hair and a beautiful bone structure. She always reminded me of the famous Jamaican freedom fighter, Nanny, who fought for the Maroons in the 18th century in the Jamaican civil war when the British were fighting the Spanish. All Jamaicans know about Nanny – she is a national hero, like the British have Winston Churchill and the Americans have Abraham Lincoln. You see all these images and drawings of this great woman, and to me she looked just like my grandmother.

Gran was a big part of the Baptist church and that is a focal point of Jamaican country life. She was a very spiritual person and used to organise the choir. I used to be so proud watching her leading the singing – it was like a rock concert in that church! Everybody would bounce up and down, cheer and clap, wail and sing their hearts out. That is where I got my first love of music, no question.

My grandfather was fantastic as well. He seemed like a superman to me. We were quite poor but my grandfather had a little land and some horses and cattle so he was like a don in Content! He grew everything we needed on his land – sugar cane, yams, bananas, mangoes and ackee (Jamaica's national fruit, which is eaten as a vegetable) – so it didn't matter that we never had money to go to the market. My grandfather grew what we needed and gave away what was left over.

I was always fascinated by how he tended his crops and nurtured the food and sometimes he would take me out in the fields with him. That was great because it made me feel as if I was doing Big Man stuff, like boys always want to. We would ride along side-by-side on his horse-drawn dray, and I would feel on top of the world. When I go back to Jamaica nowadays, one of the first places I go is to my grandfather's tomb to say hello to him. He was a real hero to me.

I only went to school for two or three days in all my time in Jamaica. It didn't occur to me to mind – my family just couldn't afford it. You had to pay for the schooling, the books, the uniforms, everything, and it was impossible for us to do that. Instead, I would spend every day outside. I used to love that – what boy wouldn't? When I got up in the morning, I would take the goats out to pasture. They would go into the cane field and I would start having my day's adventures.

When you're a country boy, it informs your whole life. You are sharper and harder than the town kids. You have to be able to run farther and faster. You get used to walking five miles where town kids can just get a bus. You learn more skills, you learn how to survive and you learn to be close to nature and appreciate where your food comes from.

I would shoot birds in the fields with my slingshot, or go out with my fishing rod. I didn't need bait – the fish were so abundant that you could just put the hook in the water, dangle it under the fish's gill, give it a jerk and pull it out! I would light a fire and cook whatever I caught on a stick. When I got home my gran would always have some food ready, but I wouldn't be hungry because I had already eaten.

My best friend Carlie and I got into all sorts of scrapes in Content. We made all our own toys. We made cars and trucks out of wood, or gigs, which were like spinning tops. We built our own draughts board and pieces and spent hours playing that, and we played cricket with a ball we made out of cork or the seed from an avocado pear which we wrapped in tar from the street.

We never had a television in Content. I had a cousin who had one, and anybody who got to see it raved about it. It was such a big deal. I only saw television twice all the time I was living in Jamaica. Once I watched horse racing, and once I watched the American cowboy show, Bonanza. It seemed like the most exotic thing in the world.

We didn't have a telephone so I couldn't talk to my parents in London. Maybe three times a year we would get a barrel full of presents from England, and when they came, it was better than Christmas Day. It would contain clothes, shoes, sugar – anything that my parents could throw together to make our lives in Jamaica a little bit better.

The barrel would always have a letter in it and my grandmother would read it out. I used to love it when she read out my name because I'd know that my mum was thinking of me. She would always send me a kiss and that made me feel good. My grandmother would always write back, but you would know that with the Jamaican postal system, it would take six months for it to arrive!

Content came alive at night. Every evening the village would gather outside Mr Butler's house and everybody would tell each other these great stories. People would bring their work with them – if they had corn to strip or tobacco to roll, they would do it and everybody would help them as they talked. That was what Content was all about.

We kids would sit listening to the conversations and quietly hero-worship the storytellers. I have no idea if the stories were true – they were certainly tall tales! One man talked about going to May Pen, which was five miles away, and having to cross a bridge that was a mile high, and I privately imagined it being ten miles high! I used to sit there soaking it all in and thinking, 'Wow, I can't wait to be an adult!'

By the time I was eight, I was my grandmother's sous chef – although I didn't know that phrase then! There was always food on the go in our house because people dropped by all the time and my grandmother would never let anybody leave without being fed. We often had a house full of guests and it got so I would know what my grandmother was going to do in the kitchen even before she did.

I don't think I ever really thought that I would leave Jamaica. In my head I knew that my parents would send for me one day, but instinctively I thought my perfect life in Content would go on forever. But then when I was 11, in 1969, a barrel arrived from England. My mum had put a black suit and some nice shoes in there for me to travel in. It was time to start my new life in London...

Turn to page 66 for more of my story.

This is where my grandparents' place once stood

EVERYDAY CARIBBEAN

Put a little spice in your life with these easy family-style recipes. Get cooking, no excuses!

Caribbean Chicken Soup

Just a small amount of chicken gives this soup a whole heap of flavour. It is packed with vegetables and is full of natural goodness.

Sprinkle the lemon juice over the chicken. Put the chicken into a duchy or large flameproof casserole with 750ml/ 1½ pints cold water, cover, bring to the boil and cook for 25 minutes.

Add the christophene, pumpkin, yam and potatoes to the pot. Bring back to the boil and cook for a further 10–15 minutes.

Add the soup mix, spring onions, chilli, thyme and salt, then reduce the heat and simmer for about 15 minutes.

Serves 8

juice of ½ lemon

1 chicken quarter, chopped into 4 pieces

½ christophene, peeled and chopped

1/16 (about 150g/5oz) pumpkin, peeled, deseeded and chopped

1 small piece (about 100g/3½oz) soft white yam, peeled and chopped

1 potato, peeled and chopped

55g/2oz sachet chicken flavour noodle soup mix

1 spring onion, finely chopped

1 small whole Scotch bonnet chilli

1 fresh thyme sprig

1 tsp salt

ROOTS RECOMMENDS:
For a bigger meal, make up some dumplings (see page 103) and add to the pot with the soup mix, spring onions, chilli, thyme and salt and simmer for 15 mins. Make sure the dumplings are cooked through before serving.

Ital Red Pea Soup

You'll see the word 'ital' in many Caribbean recipes. It comes from the word 'vital' and is the approved diet of Rastafarians.

Rinse the red kidney beans under cold running water, then put them into a large bowl and cover with 1.7 litres (3 pints) of cold water. Leave to soak overnight.

Strain the soaking water into a large pan and bring to the boil. Meanwhile, rinse the soaked beans under cold running water and throw any damaged ones away. Add the beans to the boiling water, bring back to a vigorous boil, cover and boil vigorously for 10 minutes (you have to do this to get rid of the poisonous toxins). Reduce the heat and simmer for a further 10 minutes until the beans are becoming tender.

Add the coconut cream, carrots, pumpkin, potato and christophene to the beans. Pour in 600ml (1 pint) of water, to replace what's boiled away and add the chilli and garlic. Cook over a moderate heat for a further 30 minutes.

Add the green pepper, spring onion, onion, thyme, allspice berries, all purpose seasoning, salt, black pepper, ginger and the butter and continue to cook while you make the dumplings.

Make up the dumplings according to the recipe on page 103 and roll into 15 small torpedoes. These are called spiller dumplings. Add to the pot, cover and simmer for a further 30 minutes. Serve.

ROOTS RECOMMENDS:
To make a beef soup, simply add 250g/9oz cubed stewing beef to the pot with the red kidney beans right at the beginning.

Serves 6

425g/14oz dried red kidney beans

½ packet (about 100g/3½oz) coconut cream

2 carrots, peeled and chopped

350g/12oz pumpkin, peeled and chopped

350g/12oz potato, chopped

½ christophene, peeled and chopped

1 garlic clove, chopped

1 whole Scotch bonnet chilli

¾ green pepper, deseeded and chopped

1 spring onion, green part only, chopped

1 onion, chopped

1 fresh thyme sprig

5–6 allspice berries (pimento seeds)

1 tsp salt

2 tsp all purpose seasoning

1 tsp ground black pepper

2½cm/1in piece fresh root ginger, peeled and chopped

knob of butter

Spiller Dumplings (see page 103), to serve

TIP:
If you forget to soak the red kidney beans overnight you can still use dried ones, but you'll need to boil them for 1 hour 30 minutes to make them really tender.

Salmon St Jago de la Vega

This dish is named after the town of St. Jago de la Vega, or Spanish Town, which was the capital of Jamaica from the 16th to 19th centuries.

Put the salmon fillets in a large non-metallic dish, pour over the sauce and turn the fish until coated. Cover with clingfilm and leave to marinate in the refrigerator overnight.

Brush off the excess sauce and reserve. Heat the oil in a large frying pan, add the salmon and fry over a low heat on both sides for a few minutes. Remove the fish from the pan.

Add the peppers, onion, spring onion, garlic and carrot to the pan with 200ml/7fl oz of water and mix in the reserved sauce. Push the vegetables to the side and add the salmon to the centre of the pan. Cover and simmer gently for about 5 minutes, then add the broccoli and cook for a further 5 minutes until the vegetables are tender. Serve.

Serves 2

2 salmon fillets

½ bottle Reggae Reggae Sauce or chilli barbecue sauce

4 tbsp vegetable oil

¼ red pepper, finely chopped

¼ green pepper, finely chopped

½ onion, finely chopped

1 spring onion, green end only, chopped

1 garlic clove, crushed

1 carrot, peeled and finely chopped

a few small broccoli florets

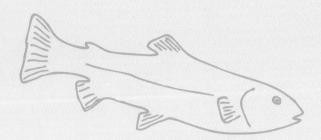

Brown Stew Fish

Many Caribbean dishes are called 'brown'. The name simply refers to the cooking method – the fish is pan-fried all over and cooked until it's browned before adding the liquid.

Rinse the snapper under cold running water, then sprinkle over the lemon juice. Put them into a large non-metallic dish and rub a little salt into the belly of each fish. Sprinkle over the all-purpose seasoning and black pepper and gently rub in. Leave to stand for at least 10 minutes, or more if you have time.

Add the oil to a large deep frying pan and heat until really hot. Add just 2 fish and fry over a high heat for about 5 minutes until lightly browned. Repeat with the other fish. Tip out the oil to leave just a thin layer in the base of the pan.

Return the fish to the pan. Add the spring onions, onion, peppers, chilli, tomatoes, thyme, garlic and 250ml/9fl oz water, then cover and cook for 10–15 minutes until the fish is cooked, the vegetables are tender and the liquid reduced.

Serves 4

4 red snapper or Jamaican tilapia, scaled, gutted and cleaned

juice of 1 lemon

$1/4$ tsp salt

1 tsp all-purpose seasoning

$1/2$ tsp coarse ground black pepper

400ml/14fl oz vegetable oil

2 spring onions, roughly chopped

1 onion, roughly chopped

1 red or yellow pepper, deseeded and sliced

1 Scotch bonnet chilli, deseeded and sliced

2 tomatoes, deseeded and chopped

2 fresh thyme sprigs

1 garlic clove, crushed

Fried Escovitch Snapper

This is similar to Brown Stew Fish, but the addition of malt vinegar gives it a kick.

Rinse the snapper under cold running water, then sprinkle over the lemon juice. Put the fish in a large non-metallic dish and rub a little salt into the belly of each fish. Sprinkle over the all-purpose seasoning and black pepper and gently rub in. Leave to stand for at least 10 minutes, or more if you have time.

Heat the oil in a large deep frying pan until really hot. Add just 2 fish and fry over a high heat for about 15 minutes until lightly browned. Remove from the pan and repeat with the other fish. Pour the vinegar into a small pan and add the onion, chillies, red and green peppers. Bring to the boil and cook for about 5 minutes.

Pour the vinegar over the fish and arrange the onions and peppers on top. Serve.

Serves 4

4 red snapper, scaled, gutted and cleaned

juice of 1 lemon

$1/4$ tsp salt

1 tsp all-purpose seasoning

$1/2$ tsp coarse ground black pepper

400ml/14fl oz vegetable oil

50ml/2fl oz malt vinegar

1 onion, sliced

2 Scotch bonnet chillies, deseeded

$1/2$ red green pepper, deseeded and sliced

$1/2$ green pepper, deseeded and sliced

Licha Fish

'Licha' is the Jamaican way of saying 'liquour'.
This dish is great way of using up left-over wine.

Rinse the fish under cold running water, then sprinkle over the lime juice and drain off any excess liquid.

Using a sharp knife, slash the fish on both sides and, using your hands, rub in salt and black pepper into all the crevices and corners.

Mix the peppers, chilli, tomato, spring onion and thyme together in a bowl, then lay 2 tablespoons of the vegetable mixture inside the fish from the head into the gut.

Heat the oil in a duchy, casserole or deep frying pan. Add any remaining mixed vegetables, the okra, chopped thyme, onion, garlic and ginger to the pan, and straightaway add the fish. Arrange the potatoes on top of the fish. Pour over about 4 tablespoons of water and season with salt and black pepper. Cover and bring to the boil, then reduce the heat and simmer gently for 10 minutes. Add the red wine, cover again and cook for a further 10 minutes. Serve.

Serves 2

2 large red snapper, scaled, gutted and cleaned

juice of 1 lime

salt and coarse ground black pepper

1 red pepper, deseeded and chopped

1 green pepper, deseeded and chopped

2 Scotch bonnet chillies, deseeded and chopped

1 tomato, deseeded and chopped

1 spring onion, green part only, chopped

1 fresh thyme sprig

3 tbsp vegetable oil

a handful of okra (about 50g/2oz)

1 fresh thyme sprig, chopped

1 onion, chopped

1 garlic clove, crushed

2.5cm/1in piece fresh root ginger, chopped

1 large potato, sliced

1 glass of red wine (about 150ml/5fl oz)

Hot Ital Stew

The key ingredient in this stew is ripe plantain, which gives it a little sweet. My grandma would have made this in a duchy, but I reckon a big wok with a lid would be cool. She used to put mud on the side of the pot to help insulate the food and make it cook quicker – this was an old tradition brought over from Africa, where they would cook on a wooden stove outside.

Smash the coconut on the ground (being careful not to hurt your toe) then crack open and drain off the coconut liquid.

Remove the 'meat' from the shell carefully with a sharp knife and grate into a bowl. Add 600ml/1 pint hot water and stir to extract the delicious hot coconut milk. If you're using creamed coconut, chop, then put into a jug and mix together with the hot water to make smooth coconut mixture.

Put the coconut milk into a pan, add the cabbage and carrots and bring to the boil. Cover, reduce the heat and simmer gently for 20 minutes, turning occasionally until the mixture turns into a sauce; this is called a coconut run-down.

Put the chillies, ginger and olive oil into a small bowl and mix together. Set aside.

Now add the grated pumpkin, plantain, onion and potato to the pan and sprinkle over the jerk seasoning, mixed herbs and allspice berries. Bring back to the boil, then reduce the heat and simmer for 15 minutes.

Add the fiery hot chilli and ginger mixture to the pan along with the broccoli, sweetcorn and butter and cook until the broccoli is just tender. Add salt to taste and serve with freshly cooked brown rice.

Serves 4

1 whole coconut or 100g/3½oz block creamed coconut

1 cabbage, the colour of your choice, shredded

2 large carrots, peeled and cut into large chunks

1–2 Scotch bonnet chillies, chopped

1cm/½in piece fresh root ginger, peeled and finely chopped

1 tbsp olive oil

250g/9oz pumpkin, deseeded and sliced (no need to peel because the skin has all the vitamins), then coarsely chopped, and grated

½ plantain, peeled and cut into chunks

1 onion, peeled and cut into large chunks

1 large Irish 'potata' (potato), cut into chunky slices

1 tsp jerk seasoning

½ tsp dried mixed herbs

3 allspice berries

4 small broccoli florets

200g can sweetcorn

knob of butter

This is a duchy!

Brown Down Chicken and Rice

Many traditional West Indian recipes brown meat
in a little oil and sugar. It gives it a rich, dark colour
and lovely flavour.

Put the chicken into a large shallow plastic container with
a lid. Stab a knife into each piece of chicken a few times,
then sprinkle the chicken seasoning and curry powder
over the chicken. Using a fork, turn the chicken over to
cover it in seasoning, then sprinkle over the soy sauce,
chopped onion and crushed garlic.

Run your thumb and forefinger down each thyme sprig
to remove the leaves. Add the leaves to the chicken and stir
everything together with a fork. Cover tightly with a lid
and shake well. If you have time, leave the chicken for a
couple of hours in the refrigerator to let all the flavours
develop, but you can use it right away.

Pour the oil into a very large pan, at least 30cm/12in wide,
with a lid, add the sugar and heat gently for about 5–7
minutes. Keep an eye on the mixture as it can burn easily,
but don't stir it. When it turns a mid-golden brown colour,
then the sugar has caramelised. Stand well back and
quickly tip the chicken into the pan, then cover with a lid
and don't touch it for 5 minutes. Turn the chicken pieces
over, cover again and cook for a further 5 minutes until
it's a lovely rich golden brown colour.

Put the rice into a measuring jug until it comes up to the
300ml/10fl oz mark, then tip it into the chicken in the pan.
Pour some water into the dish that you used to season the
chicken, then pour this into a measuring jug. You need
700ml/1¼ pints of water, and then pour this into the pan.
Cover and cook for 20 minutes over a gentle heat without
lifting the lid.

Add the black-eyed beans to the pan. Carefully stir everything
together, cover and cook for 3 minutes to warm through
the beans, then it's ready to serve.

ROOTS RECOMMENDS:
Try adding 750g/1lb 10oz of sliced potatoes to the chicken
instead of the rice.

Serves 4

500g/1lb 2oz skinless, boneless
chicken thigh fillets

1 tbsp chicken seasoning

2 tbsp Madras curry powder

2 tbsp soy sauce

1 onion, chopped

2 garlic cloves, crushed

2 fresh thyme sprigs

3 tbsp sunflower oil

2 tbsp golden granulated sugar

300g/10oz easy cook rice, rinsed

410g/14oz can black-eyed beans,
drained

Oxtail and Butter Bean Stew

Oxtail is a delicious stewing meat and is very popular in Caribbean cooking. It's great value too!

Rinse the oxtail in cold water, then pour over the vinegar and drain well.

Put the meat into a large bowl, add the salt, all-purpose seasoning, black pepper and gravy browning and mix together. Rub in the spring onions, onions, chilli and peppers and leave for 30 minutes, or overnight if you have the time.

Heat the oil in a duchy or large flameproof casserole until really hot. Add the meat and cook over a high heat for about 5–10 minutes until the meat is sealed. Keep cooking and stirring for a further 10 minutes until the meat is a good dark brown colour all over.

Pour in 600ml/1 pint water, cover, then reduce the heat and simmer very gently for about 2 hours until the meat is really tender.

Add the drained butter beans to the stew and cook for just a few minutes to warm them through. Serve.

Serves 4

8 pieces of oxtail on the bone, chopped into small pieces

150ml/5fl oz malt vinegar

salt

2 tbsp all-purpose seasoning

½ tsp coarse ground black pepper

1–2 tsp gravy browning

2–3 spring onions, chopped

3 onions, roughly chopped

1 Scotch bonnet chilli, deseeded and chopped

½ red pepper, deseeded and finely chopped

½ green pepper, deseeded and finely chopped

3 tbsp vegetable oil

400g/14oz can butter beans, drained

'Fry big fish first, little one after'

Take care of the important things first

Brown Stew Chicken with Yard-Style Gravy

This is real Jamaican home-style cooking. Nobody makes food the way we remember it from when we were back at home or 'back a yard'.

Rub the chicken all over with the lemon juice to remove traces of the skin. Put the chicken in a non-metallic dish and sprinkle over with salt, the all-purpose seasoning, black pepper and chicken seasoning. Using your hands, rub the seasonings in to give the meat a good flavour and leave in the refrigerator for 30 minutes or overnight if you have time. (Be sure to wash your hands really well after touching raw chicken and meat.)

Heat the oil in a duchy or large deep flameproof casserole until really hot.

Remove the chicken from the seasoning, reserving the seasoning mix for later. Add 6–8 pieces of chicken and fry gently for about 5 minutes on each side until the chicken is browned. Remove the chicken from the pot and carefully scoop out most of the oil, leaving just a small amount in the bottom.

Return the chicken to the pot, tip in the reserved seasoning mixture, the spring onions, onions, chilli, garlic and peppers. Pour in 450ml/16fl oz water, add the butter, then cover and simmer for 15 minutes until the liquid is reduced to a nice gravy. Serve with rice.

Serves 4–6

16 pieces of chicken (leg, thigh, breast), skinned

juice of 1 lemon

1/2 tsp salt

2 tbsp all-purpose seasoning

1/2 tsp coarse ground black pepper

2 tsp chicken seasoning or all purpose seasoning

400ml/14fl oz vegetable oil

3 spring onions, chopped

2 onions, chopped

1 Scotch bonnet chilli, deseeded and chopped

1 garlic clove, chopped

1/2 red pepper, deseeded and chopped

1/2 green pepper, deseeded and chopped

knob of butter

Levi's Rice, to serve (see page 16)

'Wha' sweet goat, a go work im belly'

The things that give you the most pleasure may also harm you

BOURBON
BEACH

JERK
CHICKEN

WE SPECIALIZE IN

Birdies Jerk

Birdie's Jer

Chicken Curry

Caribbean food has been influenced by many cultures and by people brought over to the region as indentured servants or slaves. Indian flavours have been used in Caribbean cooking since the 1930s. This is quick, easy and delicious – a great family dinner.

Rinse the chicken in cold water, then sprinkle over the lemon juice and drain off the excess liquid.

Put the chicken in a non-metallic dish and sprinkle over the salt, all-purpose seasoning, chicken seasoning, black pepper, curry powder, onions, spring onions, chilli, pepper and thyme. Using your hands, rub everything in really well. Cover and leave in the refrigerator for at least 30 minutes or overnight if you have the time.

Heat the oil in a large duchy or flameproof casserole until really hot, add the chicken and cook for 3–4 minutes to seal the meat. Add 300ml/10fl oz cold water, cover, then reduce the heat and simmer gently for 30 minutes until the chicken is tender. Serve with rice and Levi's Salad (see page 128).

Serves 4

1 chicken, skinned and chopped into 16 pieces

juice of 1 lemon

1 tsp salt

2 tbsp all-purpose seasoning

1 tsp chicken seasoning

½ tsp coarse ground black pepper

3 tbsp mild Madras curry powder

2 onions, finely chopped

2 spring onions, chopped

1 Scotch bonnet chilli, chopped and deseeded (retain seeds if you like heat!)

1 red pepper, deseeded and finely chopped

2 fresh thyme sprigs

50ml/2fl oz vegetable oil

'A no de bud wha' sing dat a mek de bes'

It's not the best singers that make the best recor

Caribbean Curry

This classic recipe traditionally uses flavoursome goat meat, which is available from Asian and Caribbean food stores, but if you are unable to find it, use neck of lamb instead.

Put the meat in a large bowl and pour over the vinegar, then sprinkle over the lime juice. Rinse in cold water and drain.

Put the meat into a clean bowl, add the all purpose seasoning, curry powder, onions, spring onions, chilli and garlic and leave to marinate in the refrigerator for at least 30 minutes. The flavour will be much better if you leave it overnight.

Heat the oil in a duchy or large flameproof casserole until really hot, add the marinated meat and stir-fry for 3-4 minutes until the meat is sealed.

Add 600ml/1 pint water, then reduce the heat, cover and cook very gently for about 1½–2 hours until the meat is really tender. Serve with rice.

Serves 4

1kg/2lb 4oz goat meat on the bone or neck of lamb, chopped

150ml/5fl oz malt vinegar

juice of 1 lime

2 tbsp all-purpose seasoning

3 tbsp mild Madras curry powder

2 onions, chopped

3-4 spring onions, chopped

1½ bell chilli, deseeded and chopped

1 garlic clove, chopped

3 tbsp vegetable oil

de bes'
nest'

Spicy Hummus Dip

Delicious for sharing, spreading, smothering, dipping. Try it on roti (see page 112) or with your favourite sandwich ingredients.

Put the chickpeas, lemon juice, oil, garlic, chilli barbecue sauce or Reggae Reggae sauce and 2 tablespoons of water into a food processor and process to a chunky purée.

Season to taste with salt and black pepper.

Transfer to a bowl and serve with vegetable crisps and carrot sticks.

Serves 10

2 x 400g/14oz cans chickpeas, drained and rinsed

100ml/3$\frac{1}{2}$fl oz lemon juice, from about 2 large lemons

80ml/2$\frac{3}{4}$fl oz olive oil

1 garlic clove, chopped

1 tbsp chilli barbecue sauce or Reggae Reggae Sauce

salt and freshly ground black pepper

To serve

vegetable crisps

carrot sticks

Reggae Beans on Toast

Perk up your baked beans with some spicy sauce, or try adding a couple of teaspoonfuls of vinegar and sugar when you warm them through.

Put the beans into a small pan and add the chilli barbecue sauce or Reggae Reggae Sauce. Warm through for a few minutes. Spoon onto warm toast and serve.

ROOTS RECOMMENDS:
Sprinkle a couple of tablespoons of grated cheese over the top.

Serves 2

400g/14oz can baked beans

2–3 tbsp chilli barbecue sauce or Reggae Reggae Sauce

4 slices of toast

Reggae Cheese on Toast

This couldn't be quicker!

Preheat the grill. Toast one side of the bread under the grill, then turn over and top the untoasted side with the Reggae Reggae Sauce, spreading over evenly.

Spoon the mayonnaise on top of the sauce. Sprinkle a generous layer of cheese over the top and grill for a few minutes until the cheese is melted and turning golden. Serve.

ROOTS RECOMMENDS:
Ready grated cheese is a great timesaver. Keep a packet in the freezer and use it from frozen. This trick saves leftover cheese from turning mouldy!

Serves 4

4 slices of toast

4 tbsp Reggae Reggae Sauce or chilli barbecue sauce

8 tbsp mayonnaise

225g/8oz grated Cheddar cheese

Levi's Curried Noodles

Turn pot noodles into hot noodles!

Bring 900ml/1½ pints of water to the boil in a large pan and add the stock cube and curry paste. Add the noodles and stir-fried vegetables and bring back to the boil, pushing the noodles down into the water.

Add the chicken tikka slices and frozen peas and cook for 3 minutes, checking that the noodles are tender and separated. Drizzle with chilli barbecue sauce or Reggae Reggae Sauce and serve immediately in bowls.

TRY THIS:
Instead of stir-fried vegetables, add 2 chopped tomatoes, 5 sliced mushrooms and 75g/3oz frozen peas.

Serves 4

1 chicken stock cube

2 tbsp korma curry paste

2 blocks (100g/3½oz) fine egg noodles

250g/9oz washed and ready to cook vegetable stir-fry (beansprouts, carrots, cabbage, onion)

135g/4½ packet cooked chicken tikka slices

50g/2oz frozen peas

2 tbsp chilli barbecue sauce or Reggae Reggae Sauce

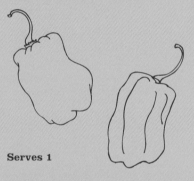

Soca Sardines on Toast

Soca music is lively Calypso music that's traditionally played at carnival. So here's how to liven up a plain old can of sardines!

Heat the oil in a frying pan, add the onion, garlic and pepper and fry for a few minutes to soften. Season with black pepper.

Add the sardines, cook for a couple of minutes and stir in the spicy tomato sauce or Love Apple Tomato Sauce. Serve on toast or with a salad.

ROOTS RECOMMENDS:
Try this with canned tuna instead of the sardines, if you like.

Serves 1

1 tbsp vegetable oil

1 onion, chopped

1 garlic clove, crushed

½ red pepper, deseeded and chopped

coarse ground black pepper

100g/3½oz can sardines in olive oil, drained

1 tbsp spicy tomato sauce or Love Apple Tomato Sauce

Spice-up Tuna and Sweetcorn Sandwich

Take a little sunshine to work or school.

Put the tuna, sweetcorn, mayonnaise and spicy tomato sauce or Love Apple Tomato Sauce in a bowl and mix together.

Split the coco bread or pitta bread and spoon in the filling, then serve.

Serves 1

100g/3½oz can tuna, drained

2 tbsp sweetcorn

1 tbsp mayonnaise

2 tsp spicy tomato sauce or Love Apple Tomato Sauce

1 coco bread or pitta bread

Corned Beef Cook-up

Here's a hot and happening store cupboard supper.

Heat the oil in a frying pan, add the onion and garlic and cook gently for a few minutes to soften.

Add the corned beef and fry for a few minutes, turning until warmed through.

Smother with spicy tomato sauce or Love Apple Tomato Sauce and serve with freshly cooked rice.

Serves 2

1 tbsp vegetable oil

1 onion, chopped

1 garlic clove, crushed

200g/7oz can corned beef, chopped

2 tbsp spicy tomato sauce or Love Apple Tomato Sauce

ROOTS RECOMMENDS:
Add a couple of cubed raw potatoes with the onion and cook for 10 minutes before adding the corned beef.

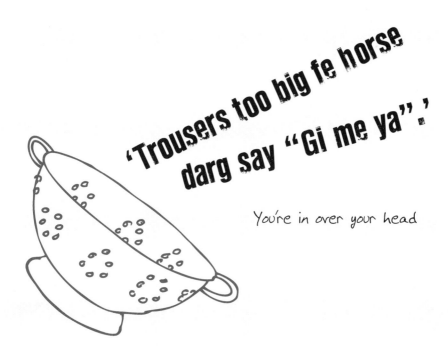

'Trousers too big fe horse darg say "Gi me ya".'

You're in over your head

Roast Sweet Potatoes

Preheat the oven to 200°C/400°F/Gas Mark 6. Fill a large bowl with cold water. Peel the potatoes and put straight into the water (otherwise they will discolour).

Cut each potato in half, so that they are all about the same size, then put them into a large pan and cover with cold water. Add a pinch of salt and cover with a lid. Bring to the boil and as soon as the water is boiling, set the timer for 5 minutes.

After 5 minutes, drain the potatoes into a colander in the sink. Shake the potatoes around in the colander to roughen up the edges. This helps guarantee super crispy roast spuds.

Pour the olive oil into a large roasting tin and put into the hot oven for 3 minutes. Tip the potatoes into the hot oil and use a spoon to spread them evenly around the tin, then sprinkle with sea salt.

Roast for 30 minutes, then, using a flat spatula, turn them over and cook for a further 15–20 minutes or until they are crisp and golden. Try serving with a roast chicken (see page 64).

Serves 4

1kg/2lb sweet potatoes
6 tbsp olive oil
sea salt

'Wanti-wanti can't. Get it and geti-geti no want it'

Nice 'n Spicy Roast Chicken with Lemon and Thyme

Make your Sunday roast rock!

Preheat the oven to 200°C/400°F/Gas Mark 6. Push the onion into the cavity of the chicken. Cut the lemon into 4 wedges and push right inside with 4 thyme sprigs, then put the chicken into a large roasting tin. Throw on the other 2 sprigs of thyme, then sprinkle the chicken seasoning, all-purpose seasoning and black pepper evenly over the top and drizzle with olive oil.

Roast the chicken for 1 hour, then spread with the chilli barbecue sauce or Reggae Reggae Sauce and cook for a final 20 minutes. (If your chicken is a different size, you can check timings by allowing 20 minutes per 500g/1lb 2oz, plus an extra 20 minutes.)

Serves 4

1 onion

1.3kg/3lb whole chicken

1 lemon

6 fresh thyme sprigs

1 tbsp chicken seasoning

2 tsp all-purpose seasoning

freshly ground black pepper

2 tbsp olive oil

4 tbsp chilli barbecue sauce or Reggae Reggae Sauce

Roast Sweet Potatoes, to serve (see page 63)

TIP: To see if the chicken is cooked, use a sharp knife to make a small cut between the chicken breast and leg at the thigh. The juices that come out should be clear; if they look pink, the chicken is not ready and needs to be cooked for longer.

COMING TO LONDON

When my parents finally called for me to join the rest of the family in London, saying goodbye to my grandmother was heartbreaking. She was everything I knew, she had been like a mother to me, and I was so tearful leaving her behind. It must have been even harder for her. She had raised all of my brothers and sisters and waved each of us off one-by-one every year, and I was the biggest wrench because I was the last.

Every time I have another success in my cooking career, I mentally thank my grandmother, because it really is all down to her. Reggae Reggae Sauce is made from her original recipe. I have amended it over the years but it would not exist without Miriam: she made me what I am, and when she died when I was 17, it was the saddest day of my life. I would like to thank her, and her kindness, for everything.

Being driven to the airport in Kingston was exciting: it was the first time I had ever been in a car, let alone an airplane! The flight was fun but, typically for me, what sticks in my mind is how bad the airplane food was! It was the first time I had ever eaten processed food and it was so horrible. I mean – baked beans? What was that about?

So in 1969 I left Paradise behind, and when my journey was over, I thought I had arrived in Hell. My hard new life hit me as soon as I landed at Heathrow. I had flown away from sunshine, greenery and smiles and I arrived in London in the middle of winter. My parents picked me up and as we drove to Brixton, I peered out of the window and saw these sad trees with no leaves. What was this place? I was in a strange land and I wanted to turn around and fly back to the warmth and security and love that I knew.

London was so different from Content and my first few months were gruelling. I loved my mum but I hadn't seen her for years. My brothers and sisters were grown up and I had a younger sister, Marcia, I had never met before. In Jamaica I was the youngest and the apple of my grandmother's eye, but in London Marcia got all the special treatment.

My father was a hard man. I didn't have a memory of him in Content because I was too young, but he turned out to be a strict Jamaican father who ruled by the band and the belt and he was tough on me. He had this two-foot strap made of leather hanging in the cellar and if I did anything he didn't like, he used it on me good and proper.

My mother put me into Tulse Hill Secondary School. At first it was awful because I hadn't any schooling in Jamaica, I came to England unable to read or write. I couldn't say my ABC and I could hardly count beyond 10. They put me in a huge class where the clever kids sat at the front and the slow ones at the back, and I was so far back that the teacher had to shout to ask me anything!

I was desperate to learn and to be at the front of the class and to know the answers to all the questions, but I would never have done it without my mother. Every evening, after school, she taught me how to read and write for hours. We'd go to the library and get out books: I used to love Enid Blyton's Famous Five adventures. Through my mother's tutelage, I learned everything that the school didn't have time to teach me.

By the second year I was right at the front of the class and enjoying it. I liked geography and art and also woodwork because I could use the skills I had learned in Content when Carlie and I were carving all our own toys out of wood. But my favourite lessons were English and music. I loved poetry and I soon started writing my own rhymes, which definitely presaged my songwriting later in my life.

As a teenager, music was everything to me. I was always in the school music room, singing and trying to write songs. My friends Quarry, Leroy and Doyley and I were eternally trying to form a band and set up gigs in the school. It didn't seem then like something I could do as a career, but music excited me more than anything else.

By then I had stopped missing Jamaica and felt like a Londoner. It was easy to mix with the kids in school because I could impress them: I was a country boy, so I was great at climbing trees, opening bottles without an opener or making catapults. I could strip a match in four with a nail, so of course the other boys liked me!

My father was a rat-catcher for Lambeth Council, which meant he worked nights, and my mum was a clippie on the buses for London Transport. Every day when I came home from school, I had to go straight into the kitchen and cook my father's food for him to take to work. He liked big traditional Caribbean meals like rice and peas (the Caribbean term for red beans). I had to always get it right because if I did anything wrong, there was always that big leather strap hanging down in the cellar!

My sister Jean would take me food shopping in Brixton market and I quickly got used to market life. I had never been to market in Kingston or May Pen in all the time I lived in Jamaica, and the first time we went to Railton Road and we saw all the food spread out everywhere, it was amazing. There was so much exciting stuff I didn't know where to look.

So by 14, I was cooking big meals like my grandmother used to. I was learning new techniques, because my mother had picked up a more English style of cooking and was using different kinds of herbs than what we had available in Jamaica. In Content, everything was fresh and home-grown but in London we used dried and packet foods and they all had different textures, which I learned to use.

Looking back, I'm glad my parents were strict because that traditional Jamaican upbringing made me grow up to be a decent and respectful person. But as a teen I wasn't perfect and I started falling away at school. After I'd learned to read and write and caught up to everybody else, I lost interest and didn't get very good results in my exams. So I left school at 16 and got a job as an engineer. I learned to use a lathe and I was a steady worker but by then my head was full of music. I couldn't think of anything except for Bob Marley and Burning Spear and Culture and all the great reggae music coming out of Jamaica. So after a year I left the factory and decided to get serious about making music.

There have been times in my life I have thought that somebody is looking after me. One of those times came just after I left the factory, when I had an encounter that changed my life...

What happened to me next? Turn to page 80 to find out.

RISE AND SHINE

Get up, stand up with a sunny
island breakfast.

Jamaican Porridge

This porridge is sweet and smooth – not like traditional porridge – give it a try!

Pour 600ml/1 pint of water into a pan and bring to the boil, then reduce the heat.

Put the oats and 200ml/7fl oz semi-skimmed milk into a bowl and mix together, then transfer to a blender and whiz until smooth.

Gradually add the oat mixture to the pan, stirring all the time, for about 5 minutes until thickened and smooth.

Add the rest of the semi-skimmed milk, the condensed milk, grated nutmeg, Caribbean essence, almond essence, vanilla essence, cinnamon and salt and warm through for a few minutes, stirring constantly. Serve warm.

Serves 4

150g/5oz organic porridge oats

600ml/1 pint semi-skimmed milk

400g/14oz can sweetened condensed milk

½ tsp freshly grated whole nutmeg or ground

1 tsp mixed Caribbean essence

1 tsp almond essence

1 tsp vanilla essence

½ tsp ground cinnamon

½ tsp salt

Cornmeal Porridge

My grandmother's trick to this porridge was to stir it up really well.

Pour 1 litre/1¾ pints water into a pan, add the cinnamon and bring to the boil.

Meanwhile, put the cornmeal in a bowl and gradually add most of the coconut or semi-skimmed milk, reserving about 100ml/3½fl oz. My grandmother taught me how to do this as it's tricky – you need to stir all the time to make a smooth paste with no lumps.

Pour the cornmeal mixture into the hot boiling water. Again, stir constantly as you pour and as the mixture thickens.

Pour in most of the condensed milk. Then, stirring all the time, add the nutmeg, Caribbean essence, almond essence, vanilla essence, cinnamon and salt. Add a little more of the reserved milk, if you like. Serve.

Serves 4

1 tsp ground or fresh cinnamon

150g/5oz fine cornmeal

600ml/1 pint coconut milk or semi-skimmed milk

400g/14oz can sweetened condensed milk

½ tsp freshly grated whole nutmeg or ground

1 tsp mixed Caribbean essence

1 tsp almond essence

1 tsp vanilla essence

½ tsp ground cinnamon

½ tsp salt

Peanut Porridge

This is a completely different type of porridge – uniquely Jamaican.

Pour 600ml/1 pint water and the coconut milk into a pan, add the cinnamon and bring to the boil.

Meanwhile, put the peanuts into a processor and whiz until finely ground. Mix 200ml/7fl oz semi-skimmed milk into the peanuts to make a smooth paste. Gradually add the ground peanuts to the pan, stirring all the time, until the mixture thickens.

Add the remaining semi-skimmed milk, the condensed milk, nutmeg, Caribbean essence, almond essence, vanilla essence, ground cinnamon and salt and warm through. When the mixture is thickened and smooth, it's ready to serve.

Serves 4

400g/14oz can coconut milk

1 tsp ground or fresh cinnamon

150g/5oz unsalted peanuts

600ml/1 pint semi-skimmed milk

400g/14oz can sweetened condensed milk

½ tsp freshly grated whole nutmeg or ground

1 tsp mixed Caribbean essence

1 tsp almond essence

1 tsp vanilla essence

½ tsp ground cinnamon

½ tsp salt

Banana Porridge

Pour 200ml/7fl oz water and the coconut milk into a pan, add the cinnamon and bring to the boil.

Meanwhile, peel the skin from the green banana and chop the flesh into very small pieces. Put the green banana into a blender and add some semi-skimmed milk. Whiz for 3–4 minutes until smooth.

Gradually stir the green banana mixture into the pan of water and coconut milk, stirring all the time for about 5 minutes until thickened and smooth.

Put the cornmeal into a bowl, add enough cold water to make a smooth paste, then pour into the thickened green bananas. Keep heating and stirring to make sure the cornmeal doesn't go lumpy, then simmer gently for 10–15 minutes, stirring from time to time until smooth.

Add the remaining semi-skimmed milk, the condensed milk, nutmeg, Caribbean essence, almond essence, vanilla essence, cinnamon and salt and cook for a few more minutes. Serve straight away.

Serves 4

5 tbsp coconut milk

pinch of ground cinnamon

1 green banana

2 tbsp fine cornmeal

100ml/3½fl oz semi-skimmed milk

100ml/3½fl oz sweetened condensed milk

pinch of freshly ground nutmeg

1 tsp mixed Caribbean essence

1 tsp almond essence

1 tsp vanilla essence

½ tsp ground cinnamon

½ tsp salt

Mash-Up Eggs

Back home, if someone says, 'I mash up my leg, I mash up my hand' it just means that they bashed their leg or hurt their hand. This is kinda the same thing – you don't want to totally scramble up those eggs and beat the hell out of them; just bruise them as they cook. A bit like how posh restaurants serve up crushed potato instead of mashed potato!

Break the eggs into a bowl. Add the milk, salt and black pepper and whisk together with a fork. Stir in the garlic, spring onions and tomato.

Pour the oil into a frying pan and tip around to coat the base, then add the butter and heat until hot.

Pour the egg mixture into the frying pan and cook over a low heat for a few minutes. As the eggs begin to set, use a spatula to move the egg mixture from the edges to the centre of the pan. Don't go too crazy; it's not scrambled eggs.

When the egg is firm, it's ready. Pour on some spicy tomato ketchup or Love Apple Sauce to taste and tuck in with some fried dumplings.

Serves 1

3 large eggs

3 tbsp milk

salt and freshly ground black pepper

½ garlic clove, finely chopped

1 spring onion, green end only, chopped

1 tomato, peeled and deseeded

1 tbsp vegetable oil

knob of butter

To serve

spicy tomato ketchup or Love Apple Tomato Sauce

Fried Dumplings (see page 21)

'De tune yuh playing no the One I dancing'

Ackee and Saltfish

Ackee is a fruit and probably one of the most expensive imported Caribbean foods. It has an amazing silky texture, bright yellow colour and there's nothing else like it. Saltfish, or salt cod, is fish that has been dried and heavily salted. It needs to be rinsed and boiled before using.

I like to chop my vegetables small so that the saltfish is the most important part – it's not vegetable stew.

Rinse the salt cod in warm water to dissolve the salt, then put into a pan and cover with warm water. Bring to the boil and boil for about 5 minutes until the salt dissolves. Drain and rinse again, then gently break up the salt cod into 2cm/³/₄in-sized pieces.

Heat 100ml/3¹/₂fl oz of the oil in a duchy or large casserole dish for a couple of minutes. Tip in the vegetables, cover and cook very gently for 10 minutes. Add the spicy tomato ketchup and cook for a further 3 minutes.

Heat the remaining oil in a frying pan, add the salt cod and cook for 5 minutes, then turn over and cook the other side.

Drain 5 tablespoons of the oil and juices from the vegetables.

Remove the salt cod from the pan and break it up into chunks. Add to the vegetables in the duchy.

Season with black pepper and add the drained ackee. Cover, but leave a small gap so you can pour off 50ml/ 2fl oz of the liquid if you need to – the finished dish should not be very runny. Leave to cook gently for a further 5 minutes until the ackee is tender and the flavour of the black pepper comes through.

Serves 4

300g/10oz skinless, boneless salt cod

200ml/7fl oz vegetable oil

2 spring onions, green ends only, chopped

1 onion, roughly chopped

¹/₂ red pepper, cored, deseeded and finely chopped

¹/₂ green pepper, cored, deseeded and finely chopped

1 Scotch bonnet chilli, deseeded (unless you want to be a real hotty) and chopped

1cm/¹/₂in piece fresh root ginger, peeled and roughly chopped

4 fresh thyme sprigs, each broken into small pieces

1 garlic clove, chopped

3 tbsp spicy tomato ketchup or Love Apple Tomato Sauce

¹/₂ tsp freshly ground black pepper

540g/1lb 5oz can ackee in salted water, drained and rinsed to remove all the salt

'PLAY I SOME MUSIC' (Bob Marley)

As a young teenager, I loved a sound system (a group of DJs and MCs) in Brixton called Sir Coxsone and I went to all their shows and dances. Lloydie Coxsone was the main man on the mic, Festus was the selector who chose the records and if you loved reggae back then, they were big news – the Fatboy Slim of 1970s Brixton!

One fateful morning, I was walking through Brixton to sign on with three former school friends called Blacker, Lloyd and Dufus. We saw Festus from Sir Coxsone struggling to load a massive speaker box into a van and ran over to help him. Festus thanked us, said Coxsone were playing Wolverhampton that night and invited us to go with them.

He didn't need to ask twice! We excitedly ran home to get a change of clothes and crammed into the back of Coxsone's van for a four-hour journey to Wolverhampton. We loved it so much in the back of that van that, on and off, I spent the next 25 years there.

The Coxsone Sound System became my second family. Lloydie Coxsone organised it in the same way Berry Gordy ran Motown. He would try to school the youth of Brixton with his sound system so they could move into music and become singers or DJs. It was all I had ever wanted and I grabbed it with both hands.

Coxsone played right across London: I remember a club called Bennett's in Battersea which was owned by Lord Snowdon, Princess Margaret's husband, and had piranha fish under the dance floor. The Coxsone sound system even played regularly in the West End in a club called the Roaring Twenties in Carnaby Street.

Through Coxsone, I also started going to Notting Hill Carnival. We played it every year from about 1975 and the very first time I set eyes on the Carnival, it blew me away. I loved the music, the food, the colours: it was just a great annual party where you could do whatever you wanted for two whole days.

Nowadays, Notting Hill Carnival is very calypso based and covers all things Caribbean, but back then the flavour was pure Jamaican. The stallholders were blasting out reggae, selling jerk chicken and shouting out their wares. I'd never been to a festival in Jamaica in all my time in Content, and I thought it was wonderful.

I loved the first day of Carnival best, with all the kids dressed up on the floats along a certain theme. One year the theme was Anansi, who in Jamaican folklore is a human spider, so all the kids were in spider costumes. It was fun – but Coxsone was very serious about Carnival.

Before it began, we would spend a lot of money on our speakers, paint them and get all the latest sounds. We all got dressed up and tried to be the heaviest and loudest sound system at Carnival. We would have fantastic sound clashes: Coxsone versus Fatman, or Coxsone versus Jah Shaka.

Festus was the main selector in Coxsone and a smooth-talking guy called Denzel was the MC, who talked or 'toasted' over the tracks. Initially I would just watch them, but Lloydie could see I had a way with words and he soon started encouraging me.

When we played dancehalls, he would let me get on the mic at the end of the evening, when there were only a few people left. I carefully honed my skills on the mic because my friend Blacker and I were longing to replace Denzel and Festus. Eventually, we did!

We didn't make much money from Coxsone but it had a lot of perks. We were playing the tunes people loved and we lived like rock stars. We got into all the clubs for free, we were cool guys living a fantastic life and we got the girls, because they loved being seen with us.

Ah yes, the girls. When I was with Coxsone, girls were always there for me because I was famous. I was a little too loose and it never occurred to me to be careful, but I have seven great kids as a result and they are the best thing in my life.

My eldest daughter, Bernice, was born when I was 19 and my son Zaion not long afterwards. I've also got Natalie, Joanne, Sharlene, Danai and Tyran and I'm proud of the fact that we all love each other and get on – we are a proper family.

But Coxsone was my family back then and we all lived together in a squat in Brixton. I still had my room at my mum's house (she keeps it for me even now!) but I was mostly at the squat. We all had our roles: I did all the cooking. If Coxsone were on the road, I would always have a pot of food going in the dressing room while they were doing a sound check.

I wrote songs that were politically conscious. As I began my music career, I didn't know who I was. We had studied history at school but it never mentioned black people: it was like we didn't exist. I remember how shocked I was when I discovered that my people had once been slaves!

We were young black kids searching for ourselves and when I heard the reggae music coming out of Jamaica, it explained a lot. As a kid I had sometimes seen Rastafarians in the street and they seemed exciting and exotic, but when I left school and listened to people like Bob Marley singing songs like Buffalo Soldier, the pieces all fell into place:

Rastafarianism is crucial to me but I don't see it as just a religion – it's a way of life. To me, it's all about knowing who you are and about appreciating your own identity. When I understood that, I began to address my character – and I started with my name.

'If you know your history
Then you know where you're coming from...'

My birth name, Keith Graham is Scottish, and though Scotland is a lovely place I have never felt Scottish! So I decided to take a new name. In the Bible, Levi is a priest, a scholarly man who administers to everyone, and that made sense to me: I always had a pen in my hand, and I was always cooking and looking after people around me. As for Roots... well, that is the strongest part of the tree.

So Levi Roots became my new name when I was on the microphone with Coxsone. Soon I was recording my first song with them. Lloydie Coxsone had a dub version (a track with the vocals taken off) of a track by a guy called Fred Locks, and he wanted me to toast over it.

I will never forget that day! I was at home making love to my girlfriend and Lloydie knocked on my door and said, 'Studio, Levi Roots!' I got up, got dressed and ran out of there!

We recorded the track and Lloyd put it out on his own Tribesman label as 'Poor Man's Story' by Levi Roots and Fred Locks. It got played on the radio and was an instant hit. It soon became a legendary tune in British reggae and I made the first money that I ever got through music.

At the same time I knew that I didn't want to just be a DJ, or a toaster. I looked at the music industry and saw that singers were around a lot longer than the people who just talked over the tracks. So I decided to form a band and try to do some real damage in the music industry.

I formed a band called Matic16. We had a full brass section and a real big sound. One time we played a gig in Brixton and Earl Morgan, the bass player from UB40, came and saw us. UB40 asked us to go out with them on their first tour. My brass section joined UB40 and travelled the world for years, earning millions, but I didn't go – because by then, I was in jail...

Turn to page 92 for the next part of my story.

Callaloo and Saltfish

This is another delicious and traditional Jamaican breakfast. Callaloo is Jamaican spinach and is available both fresh and canned from supermarkets and speciality food stores. If you cannot find it, then use frozen chopped spinach.

Rinse the salt cod in warm water to dissolve the salt, then put into a pan and cover with warm water. Bring to the boil and boil for about 5 minutes until the salt dissolves. Drain and rinse again, then gently break up the salt cod into 2cm/¾in-sized pieces.

Heat the oil in a duchy or large flameproof casserole with a lid for a couple of minutes, then tip in the onion, peppers, chilli, ginger, thyme, garlic and tomato. Cover and cook very gently for 10 minutes.

Add 1 tablespoon of spicy tomato ketchup or Love Apple Sauce and cook for a further 3 minutes.

Drain the callaloo and rinse to remove the salt, then drain again. Add to the pan, stir for a couple of minutes, then add the remaining tablespoon of tomato ketchup, if you like.

Season with black pepper. Cover, but leave a gap so you can evaporate or ladle off about 50ml/2fl oz of the liquid – the finished dish should not be very runny. Leave to cook gently for a further 5 minutes until the flavour of the black pepper comes through. Try serving with fried dumpling.

Serves 4

300g/10oz skinless, boneless salt cod

100ml/3½fl oz vegetable oil

1 onion, roughly chopped

½ red pepper, cored, deseeded and finely chopped

½ green pepper, cored, deseeded and finely chopped

1 Scotch bonnet chilli, deseeded (unless you want to be a real hotty) and chopped

1cm/½in piece fresh root ginger, peeled and roughly chopped (not too small, so that if someone doesn't like it they can see it)

4 fresh thyme sprigs, each broken into small pieces

1 garlic clove, chopped

1 small tomato, deseeded and roughly chopped (we call this a 'love apple')

1–2 tbsp spicy tomato ketchup or Love Apple Tomato Sauce

540g/1lb 5oz can callaloo (drained weight about 342g/11¾oz)

½ tsp coarse ground black pepper

'Ol ooman a swear fe callalu callalu a swear fe' ol ooman'

If you look after me, I'll look after you

Morning Mango and Passion Fruit Smoothie

Guaranteed to wake you up!

Put the mango, banana and passion fruit juice into a blender and whiz everything together until smooth. Pour into a glass to serve.

ROOTS RECOMMENDS:
Use tropical fruit juice if you can't find passion fruit juice.

Serves 1

1 ripe mango, peeled and flesh removed from the stone

1 banana, sliced

150ml/5fl oz passion fruit juice

Get Up Guava, Papaya and Banana Smoothie

Put the papaya, banana and guava juice into a blender and whiz everything together until smooth. Pour into a glass to serve.

ROOTS RECOMMENDS:
Use tropical fruit juice if you can't find guava juice.

Serves 1

1 ripe papaya, peeled, halved, deseeded and flesh chopped

1 banana, sliced

150ml/5fl oz guava juice

Pineapple Banana and Orange Sunshine Smoothie

Put the pineapple, banana and orange juice into a blender and whiz everything together until smooth. Pour into a glass to serve.

Serves 1

225g/8oz fresh or canned pineapple pieces

1 banana, sliced

150ml/5fl oz orange juice

Reggae Reggae Bloody Mary

Great for a grown-up Jamaican brunch!

Pour the vodka, tomato juice and Reggae Reggae sauce into a tumbler and mix together.

Add the crushed ice, then sprinkle with celery salt and place a celery stick in the glass to finish.

Serves 1

50ml/2fl oz vodka

100ml/3½fl oz tomato juice

1 tbsp Reggae Reggae Sauce or hot sauce like Tabasco

1 glassful of crushed ice (about 150ml/5fl oz)

pinch of celery salt

1 celery stick

Morning Carrot Juice

This is a creamy carroty drink – very rich!

Put the carrots into a large bowl and pour over 1 litre/1¾ pints water. Cover and leave for at least 1 hour.

Strain the carrots and pour the liquid into a large jug. Add the condensed milk, evaporated milk, Angostura bitters, vanilla essence, Caribbean essence and nutmeg. Chill and serve over crushed ice.

TIP: For an italversion leave out the condensed and evaporated milks, chop the carrots and boil in half the water until tender. Cool, do not strain and blend with the juice of 3 limes, 4 tbsp soft brown sugar and 50g/2oz fresh grated root ginger until smooth. Add the remaining 500ml of water and the juice of 3 more limes. Mix everything together and chill until served

Serves 6

250g/9oz carrots, peeled and grated

400g/14oz can sweetened condensed milk

175g/6oz evaporated milk

dash of Angostura bitters

½ tsp vanilla essence

¼ tsp mixed Caribbean essence

pinch of ground nutmeg

crushed ice, to serve

HARD TIMES, BIG LESSONS

I had never been a real bad boy on the streets – my Rastafarianism kept me away from that but life in Brixton back then was tense. The sus laws made sure of that. These laws allowed police to stop and search without question, and often led to people being arrested for doing absolutely nothing, sometimes just for standing around. I could never even get in my car and go anywhere because I knew I would get stopped and searched. It made a lot of people angry and permanently on the verge of doing something crazy. So, when the Brixton riots came along, I was in the wrong place at the wrong time and I got put away for it.

All I was guilty of was standing outside a café. I was minding my own business when the police suddenly charged down the street. They grabbed me, arrested me, and I got charged with assault on a police officer. That was what it was like: they arrested you, and then worked out what to charge you with! I pleaded not guilty but got sent to Pentonville for six months.

I didn't want to be in prison, of course, but although I shouldn't have been there it wasn't that bad. In some ways, life on the streets prepares you for it. If I wanted to, while I was in there I could have learned to be even more of a bad boy from real criminals who want to teach you all the tricks. Luckily, I had no interest in that.

When I came out of jail I got Matic16 back together and did my first bit of entrepreneurship – I formed a record label, Conqueror Records. My first release was a song called 'Say You Want Me' that I had written in prison for my girlfriend at the time. I also discovered a new artist called Mikey General, who is now a big star in Jamaica.

These were the halcyon days of reggae, and through Coxsone and Conqueror, I was lucky enough to work with some of the most legendary names in music: people like Sugar Minott, Junior Reid, Dennis Brown and Gregory Isaacs. I also hung out with the biggest superstar in reggae: Bob Marley.

When Bob was in London he would come to Coxsone's club in Carnaby Street. He would also play football with us in Battersea Park every Sunday. Bob was always very passionate about everything and that included football. If he hadn't been a singer, he was good enough to have played professionally. He was a short, stocky, tough-tackling midfield general: just imagine Paul Ince with dreadlocks!

I still wasn't making money through music but I loved doing it – but then my life suffered another setback. By 1986 I had started running a youth club in Brixton called The Papine. The police raided it and claimed they found drugs there – and although I was innocent, I was back inside again.

I went to Brixton jail, then Wandsworth, then Maidstone, then the Isle of Sheppey. This is not the place to talk too much my time in jail; that is for another book. But that experience totally changed my life around – and in some bizarre ways, it was the best time of my life.

I have been lucky enough that at various times in my life, I have met people kind enough to be a mentor to me and guide me on the path of righteousness. One such woman was Theresa, who was an arts liaison teacher who visited Isle of Sheppey prison. She taught me about poetry, art and Shakespeare and helped me to mend my ways. I read books, studied hard and finally got a real education.

While I was in prison, I formed a band and played gigs called Jailhouse Rock and ran the prison newspaper, The Bird. They even let me have a job outside the prison working at a children's crèche, so every day I'd take a bus from the jail to work, then go back again at night. The warders there loved me: they even named the prison library after me!

I kept applying for parole and because I was a model prisoner, I knew they would give it to me if I said that I was sorry for my crime, but I never did because I was innocent. I couldn't tell that lie. But when I came out, I knew I was never going back.

When I left jail my head was bursting with ideas because Theresa had convinced me that I was capable of anything. I'd written a book full of songs in jail and more than anything I wanted to get back into music. But before that, my career took another unexpected turn: I opened a clothes shop!

My brother owned an empty shop in Acre Lane in Brixton and he gave me the keys to it. He hadn't been looking after it so it was really dusty and horrible: I went in with a chamois and Mr Sheen and cleaned it for days. Lloydie Coxsone owned a food shop next door, and he still sometimes talks about watching me going crazy with a chamois and Mr Sheen! I called it the High Fashion Boutique, started buying in clothes for it and in no time it was a success.

Notting Hill Carnival was still a big part of my life, as it always will be. The African National Congress always sponsored the Coxsone float at Carnival and I was proud of that because Nelson Mandela was a huge hero to me. I'll never forget watching him being released from prison on TV while I was in jail myself. Then In 1992, something amazing happened: I got to sing to him on his birthday.

Mandela was visiting a recreation centre in Brixton with Prince Charles and there were tens of thousands of people outside waiting to see him. I was one of them, just another face in the crowd, but a security guard that I knew spotted me and beckoned me to the front.

The crowd passed me through the air over their heads until I was outside the centre. The organisers had a cake for Mr Mandela and as he came down the stairs to be presented with it, I sang 'Happy Birthday, Mr President' to him. I guess I was Brixton's Marilyn Monroe (although not many people would call me that!).

High Fashion was thriving but my brother who owned the shop demanded it back. We had a big fight and I just walked away from the shop, but the fight ended that day because I knew my mother wouldn't have been able to bear her two sons fighting. I made the sacrifice – but it really angered me.

After I had my fight with my brother, I cut off all my hair. A Rasta man's hair is sacred to him, but it was like I was taking the big argument out on myself by damaging what was valuable to me. I wanted to go a completely different direction in life, so – believe it or not – I put on a slick suit and became a financial adviser even though I had no experience in that field and no letters after my name. For a while I enjoyed selling mortgages because it was a chance to develop another side of myself. I guess by then I felt I could do anything in the world, and this was just another way of proving it.

After two years, though, my old life was calling me. 'Poor Man's Story' was a hit once more because Radio 1's Judge Jules had remixed it, my tunes were being bounced around again, and I decided to get back to what I knew best – music and food…

Turn to page 120 to read all about the birth of Reggae Reggae Sauce!

'When kitchen dresser fall down, mauger dars laugh'

When something bad happens,
good fortune often comes out of it

CARNIVAL

Carnival is the heart and soul of
the Caribbean. Get the party started
with these Jamaican favourites!

'Nuff Corn Soup'

There's 'nuff corn in this, man; enough for anyone. The fresh corn on the cob adds texture and the canned corn gives flavour. Corn in every mouthful.

Bring 2 litres/3½ pints water to the boil in a large pan and add the corn pieces. Add the potato, bring back to the boil and cook for 45 minutes until the corn is really tender and the potato is disintegrated. Use a potato masher to crush the potatoes if needed, as this will make the soup nice and thick and give it body.

Now add the tinned sweetcorn, the carrots, christophene, dried coriander, thyme, onion, garlic (if using), peppers, chilli and allspice. Bring to the boil, add salt to taste and the black pepper, then reduce the heat and simmer for 20 minutes until the vegetables are tender.

Serves 4

2 corn on the cobs, husks removed and each cob cut into 4 pieces

2 large potatoes, each cut into 4 pieces

200g/7oz can sweetcorn, drained and rinsed

3 small carrots, peeled and roughly chopped

½ christophene, peeled and chopped into small pieces

1 tsp dried coriander leaves

2 fresh thyme sprigs

1 onion, finely chopped

1 garlic clove, chopped (optional)

¼ red pepper, finely chopped

¼ green pepper, finely chopped

1 whole Scotch bonnet chilli

5–6 allspice berries (pimento seeds)

salt

1 tsp coarse ground black pepper

'Me throw me corn a door, me no call no fowl. Suppose yuh want to pick it up, it your business'

Mind your own business!

Fish Soup

In Jamaica, this flavoursome broth may be eaten as a chunky soup or put through a sieve. It is often called 'fish tea'.

Rinse the fish head really thoroughly under cold running water.

Fill a duchy or large casserole dish with 2 litres/3½ pints water and bring the water to the boil. Add the fish head, pumpkin, christophene, potato, chilli and allspice berries.

Bring back to the boil and cook for 30 minutes for the pumpkin, potato and fish head to soften. Press down with a potato masher.

Rinse the banana (do not peel), and slice thinly. Add it along with the diced yam to the pot. Bring to the boil again and boil for a further 15 minutes. Press everything down with a potato masher.

Add the garlic, spring onions, onion and thyme, then stir in the noodle soup mix and stock cube. Simmer for a further 10 minutes. Season to taste with salt and black pepper and add Spiller Dumplings, if you like. Eat as it is or strain to remove all the pieces.

Serves 4

1 large fish head - salmon is ideal for adding flavour

150g/5oz pumpkin, peeled and chopped

1 chrisophene, peeled and chopped

1 large regular potato, peeled and chopped

1 whole Scotch bonnet chilli

6 allspice berries

1 green banana

150g/5oz yam, peeled and chopped

1 garlic clove

2 spring onions, chopped

1 onion, chopped

1 fresh thyme sprig

1 packet vegetable noodle soup

1 vegetable stock cube, crumbled

Spiller Dumplings, to serve (optional)

Spiller Dumplings

My Grandma called these finger-length torpedo-shaped dumplings 'Spiller Dumplin's'. I don't know where the name came from but I've kept it.

Put the flour and salt into a large bowl and gradually stir in 150ml/5fl oz water until a firm dough forms. Knead until smooth.

Divide the dough into 8 pieces and roll each into a ball, then flatten each one with the palm of your hand.

Add the dumplings to soups and simmer for 15 minutes until cooked through.

Makes 8

300g/10oz plain flour
1 tsp salt

Seriously Special Reggae Boat Fish

I use sea bass because it's a fantastic fish – very succulent yet firm with plenty of meat. In Jamaica I would use snapper, so if you prefer, use this instead. Here's how to remove the gut and create an impressive boat shape just how my grandmother taught me to do. We would then bung all the vegetables and herbs into the centre – you can do the same thing. Jamaicans are seriously into fish and okra: 'Fish and festival is the boom'.

Rinse the fish under cold running water. To scale the fish, hold by the tail over some newspaper and run a knife down the fish all the way round to remove the scales. Do this carefully, making sure not to damage it in any way. Rinse the fish well under cold running water. Alternatively, you can ask your fishmonger to scale the fish for you.

To gut the fish into the special boat shape, insert the point of a sharp knife halfway into the fish, starting near the head on the outside (not from the belly in the way fish is usually gutted). Feel along the bone with your knife and press down, cutting the flesh and using the bone as a guide. Be careful not to push the knife too far in (see the step-by-step pictures on the next page).

Insert the knife again on the other side of the head, pressing the top side against the bone and cutting along the fish flesh. Now you should have two pockets within the fish, on either side of the bone.

Now with your kitchen scissors cut away the central part of the bone as near to the head as possible, leaving the head and tail intact. Keep this central slice of the fish, remove the bone, and you can use it separately.

Open up the fish, hold the head with one hand and pull the gut and entrails out with the other hand. Insert your fingers into the gill area to open it up and then completely

continued on the next page...

Serves 2

500g/1lb 2oz whole sea bass or snapper

¼ tsp ground black pepper

¼ tsp salt

1 tbsp olive oil

1 large fresh thyme sprig

1 large spring onion, green end only, chopped

1cm/½in piece fresh root ginger, peeled and sliced

½ garlic clove or more if you like it, roughly chopped

1 small carrot, peeled and cut into lengthways slices

¼ onion, roughly sliced

2 okra, ends cut off and sliced lengthways in half

⅛th of cristophene, peeled and sliced lengthways (or you could replace this with 50g/2oz regular potatoes)

1 Scotch bonnet chilli, deseeded and sliced into rings

1 tsp sweet chilli dipping sauce or Fiery Guava Dipping Sauce

cut away the gills and snip off the gills on the outside of the gills. Thoroughly rinse and clean the fish under cold running water to remove all traces of the insides.

Season the fish with salt and black pepper, including the central slice, and put it onto a large sheet of foil. Brush the fish, inside and out, with olive oil to keep it moist.

Start with the most flavoursome ingredients first: push in the thyme, then bash and bruise the spring onion to release the flavour and lay in the base of your boat. Arrange the ginger slices in the fish and push right into the head. Arrange the garlic on top, then arrange the carrots in the boat. Always thinking about how the finished fish will look. Scatter over the onion and arrange the okra and christophene or potatoes inside. Finish with the chilli rings.

The boat is almost ready to sail – we just need to add the fire – so smother over the sweet chilli dipping sauce or Fiery Guava Dipping Sauce. You can close up the fish with wooden skewers, which have been presoaked in water for 30 minutes, or my grandma would have sewn it up. Completely enclose the fish in the foil, making sure to keep the boat shape – reggae gondala style.

Either preheat the oven 180°C/350°F/Gas Mark 4 or cook the parcel on top of a hot barbecue for about 30 minutes until the fish and vegetables are tender – really special. Serve with festival or cream crackers. Get stuck in and don't waste the head; it's totally clean and really juicy if you suck it.

Cook-up Fish

If you don't have time to make Reggae Boat Fish (see pages 105–6) then this easy alternative has a lot of the same flavours and is equally delicious.

Rinse the fish, sprinkle over the lime juice and drain. Pat the fish dry thoroughly inside and outside with kitchen paper. Slash the fish flesh a couple of times on each side with a sharp knife.

Put the fish in a non-metallic dish. Mix together the all-purpose seasoning, allspice, mixed dried herbs, salt and black pepper in a small bowl, then use to season the fish inside and out.

Heat the oil in a frying pan, add the fish and fry for 3 minutes on each side. Remove from the pan.

Add the onion, thyme, garlic and red pepper to the pan. Cover and cook very gently, for about 4 minutes. Keeping the pan covered helps to keep the vegetables moist.

Add 4 tablespoons of water to the pan, then add the okra. Push the vegetables to the side of the pan, then add the semi-cooked fish into the centre. Spoon the vegetables over the fish, cover the pan and cook for a further 7 minutes.

Lift the lid and add the large pieces of crackers. Cover and return to the heat for a further 4 minutes before serving.

Serves 2

2 whole red snapper or mackerel, scaled, gutted and cleaned

juice of 1 lime

1 tsp all-purpose seasoning

1 tsp ground allspice (pimento)

1 tsp mixed dried savory, marjoram, oregano, thyme, rosemary, basil and tarragon

1 tsp salt

1 tsp ground black pepper

1 onion, sliced

2 fresh thyme sprigs, chopped

1 garlic clove, crushed

½ red pepper, deseeded and sliced

10 okra, each cut into 3 pieces

4 tbsp vegetable oil

5 cream crackers or Jamaican crackers (water biscuits), each broken into 3 or 4 pieces

ROOTS RECOMMENDS:
The combination of dried savory, marjoram, oregano, thyme, rosemary, basil and tarragon is often called 'Herbes de Provence' and is widely available in supermarkets.

Saltfish Fritters

These are great for breakfast or to nibble on for instant energy when you're jammin' away at the carnival.

Scrape the excess salt off the fish with a knife and then rinse in warm water. Put into a pan, bring to the boil and cook for 2–3 minutes.

Put the flour into a large bowl and add the spring onions and chilli.

Drain the salt cod and rinse again, then break the fish into small pieces and add to the flour mixture. Pour in 200ml/7fl oz cold water and, using a spoon, stir until the batter easily pours off the spoon, adding about 50ml/2fl oz more water, if needed.

Heat the oil in a large, deep frying pan, add 6 separate spoonfuls of the mixture to the oil and cook for about 7 minutes, then turn over and cook for a further 7 minutes until pale golden and crispy. Drain and serve.

Serves 6

275g/9½oz skinless, boneless salt cod

275g/9½oz self-raising flour

2 spring onions, finely chopped

1 Scotch bonnet chilli, deseeded and chopped

600ml/1 pint vegetable oil, for deep-frying

Stew Beef

The most important thing in this dish is the seasoning – there's nothing fancy here, this is just the way my grandmother taught me.

Put the beef into a bowl, sprinkle with the black pepper and salt, and using your hands, mix together well. You don't need anything else. Cover and leave in the refrigerator for 30 minutes, or overnight if you have the time, to allow the seasoning to really flavour the meat.

Heat the oil in a duchy or large flameproof casserole until it's medium hot. Tip in the beef to cover the base of the pan and fry on one side until browned, then turn each piece over to brown the other side and to seal in the juices. Reduce the heat and continue to cook for 15 minutes.

Now, put the spring onions, garlic, ginger, onion, peppers, tomato and thyme into another pan and add the beef in its oil. Pour in 250ml/8fl oz water, add the chilli barbecue sauce or Reggae Reggae Sauce and salt, then cover and simmer for a further 45 minutes over a gentle heat until the meat is tender. Serve with rice or wrap in a split pea roti (see page 112).

Serves 4

500g/1lb 2oz stewing beef, cut into 2.5cm/1in cubes

2 tbsp ground black pepper

1 tbsp salt

5 tbsp vegetable oil

2 large spring onions, green ends only, chopped

1 garlic clove, roughly chopped

1cm/½in piece fresh root ginger, peeled and chopped

1 onion, roughly sliced

½ red pepper, deseeded and roughly chopped

½ green pepper, deseeded and roughly chopped

1 tomato, cut into wedges

few fresh thyme sprigs, broken into pieces

2 tbsp chilli barbecue sauce or Reggae Reggae Sauce

1 tsp salt

4 split pea roti, to serve (buy ready made or see page 112 if you fancy making your own)

'Pot full, pot cover get some'

Good fortune spreads to those close to you

Split Pea Roti

These take a bit of practice to get right, but they're well worth the effort. These roti can be used to wrap up curry (see the picture on page 110).

Put the peas, turmeric, cumin, garlic and 1 teaspoon salt into a small pan. Add 200ml/7fl oz water and bring to the boil. Reduce the heat and simmer for 30 minutes or until the peas are soft, adding a little more water, if needed. Set aside to cool.

Put the flour, baking powder and the rest of the salt into a large bowl. Add the oil and gradually mix in enough milk to form a smooth dough. Knead on a floured surface for a couple of minutes. Cover with a damp tea towel and leave to rest for 30 minutes.

Put the cooled peas and 1 tablespoon of water into a food processor and whiz until smooth.

Divide the dough into 8 portions. Sprinkle the worktop with flour and roll out each piece to make 20cm/8in rounds. Spread 4 of the rounds with the pea mixture, then top with the other rounds and press to seal the edges.

Heat a heavy-based frying pan, then brush each roti with a little oil and fry in batches for 1 minute on each side or until lightly browned.

Serves 4

125g/4½oz yellow split peas, soaked in cold water overnight

¼ tsp ground turmeric

1 tsp ground cumin

1 garlic clove, finely sliced

1½ tsp salt

225g/8oz plain flour, sifted, plus extra for dusting

1½ tsp baking powder

1 tbsp vegetable oil

125–150ml/4½–5fl oz milk

a little vegetable oil for frying

Crab and Callaloo Soup

Callaloo is pretty easy to find in the speciality aisle of the supermarket, but if you can't find it, then fresh spinach is just fine.

Heat the oil in a duchy or large saucepan, add the spring onions, garlic and thyme and cook for a couple of minutes to soften.

Add the callaloo or spinach, okra, chilli and 1 litre/ 1½ pints water. Season generously with salt and black pepper and simmer for 15 minutes, stirring from time to time.

Add the crabmeat and creamed coconut and cook for a further 10 minutes or so. Squeeze in the lime juice and serve.

Serves 4

1 tbsp vegetable oil

2 spring onions, chopped

1 garlic chopped, chopped

1 fresh thyme sprig, leaves removed from the stem

350g/12oz callaloo or spinach, washed and stalks trimmed

225g/8oz okra, topped, tailed and sliced

1 whole Scotch bonnet chilli

salt and freshly ground black pepper

225g/8oz crabmeat

50g/2oz creamed coconut, grated

juice of 2 limes

Fried Fish

This simple dish is quick and easy to prepare and always goes down well.

Cut the fish into 4 cutlets (or ask your fishmonger to).

Sprinkle the all-purpose seasoning over and dip in the seasoned flour.

Heat the oil in non-stick frying pan, then carefully lower into the hot oil. Fry gently over a medium heat for 5 minutes on each side until cooked through.

VARIATION

For a lip-smackin' alternative, cook the fish as above, then heat 2 teaspoons of oil in a pan, add 1 sliced onion, ½ deseeded and sliced green pepper and 2 spring onions, green ends only, chopped. Add 2 tablespoons of malt vinegar and warm through for a couple of minutes to soften the vegetables, then pour over the fish.

Serves 2

2 trevally or Jamaican tilapia, scaled, gutted and cleaned

1 tsp all-purpose seasoning

25g/1oz flour seasoned with salt and pepper

4 tbsp vegetable oil

'Fret dem a fret and dem no get nuting yet'

Don't worry unnecessarily

The Best Fried Chicken

Everyone's got their own recipe that they swear by.
Make sure the meat is dry before you add the flavourings
and then try and chill it overnight before cooking. This
way you'll get an authentic spicy hit with every mouthful.

Rinse the chicken drumsticks and pat dry with kitchen paper.
This is crucial so they do not stick to the pan.

Put the chicken in a non-metallic dish. Mix the all-purpose
seasoning, allspice, mixed dried herbs, salt and black
pepper together in a small bowl and use to coat the chicken.
Cover and chill for 2–3 hours or overnight, if you've time.

Preheat the oven to 190°C/375°F/Gas Mark 5. Heat the oil
for deep-frying in a duchy, large deep saucepan or deep-fat
fryer until a cube of bread dropped into the hot oil browns
in 30 seconds. Add a couple of pieces of chicken at a time
and deep-fry for about 10 minutes until the chicken is
golden brown on the outside and cooked through. Keep
the chicken warm in the oven until you're ready to serve
it. This also makes sure it's thoroughly cooked through.

Serves 6

6 large chicken drumsticks

1 tsp all-purpose seasoning

1 tsp ground allspice (pimento)

1 tsp mixed dried savory,
marjoram, oregano, thyme,
rosemary, basil and tarragon
(Herbes de Provence)

1 tsp salt

1 tsp ground black pepper

600ml/1 pint vegetable oil

ROOTS RECOMMENDS:
Poke a skewer into a drumstick to check
it's cooked through – the juices should run clear.

NOTTING HILL CARNIVAL

By the mid 1990s, I was already combining my twin loves of music and food at Notting Hill Carnival. I had taken the decision to start selling my own food from a stall at the Carnival, and there was only ever really one name I could give this new venture: Levi Roots' Rasta'raunt.

All through Carnival, when I wasn't on the mic with Coxsone, my kids and I cooked up jerk chicken and mutton and ladled my grandmother's secret sauce all over it. The Rasta'raunt was packed out because it was proper Caribbean culture. Soon people were telling us that we made the best food at Carnival.

My music career was also taking off. I released my first album, 'Free Your Mind', in 1998 and it was a huge hit. I got nominated for a MOBO award for best reggae album and although I didn't win, it was a great honour.

I toured the world and had amazing experiences. The Levi Roots band played in Manhattan and at an oasis in the desert outside the Sierra Nevada. We entertained 30,000 people at a big event in Serbia and toured South Africa and Kenya with Lucky Dube, South Africa's biggest reggae artist.

Going to Africa was very special for me – it felt so much like Jamaica. We played at a racetrack in Nairobi and the crowd stretched as far as the eye could see. I'll never forget that night: I had to have oxygen on stage because I was doing my normal show, jumping around like crazy, and the altitude was so high that I couldn't breathe properly!

Yet every year, summer was all about Notting Hill. The Carnival is the last weekend in August, and from the middle of June, my kids and I would be cooking up my grandmother's sauce at home, then taking it to Carnival in big pots to ladle over the food....

By now, literally hundreds of people were coming to the Rasta'raunt and asking what was in the sauce. All the other stallholders wanted to know why our food was tastier than theirs! I didn't tell them because that was my big secret: I knew it was the sauce that made our food better.

Then around the millennium, my music fortunes began to fall away. There were a lot of protests about certain Jamaican singers whose lyrics were misogynistic or anti-gay. My music was nothing at all like that but sadly all reggae stars suffered and it became hard to get gigs.

I was trying to write a new album but the wolf was at my door so I took a driving job to earn money. If nothing else, it helped to focus my mind. In 2006, as Notting Hill approached, I decided to take many friends' advice and try to start a business around my sauce and cooking. Nothing ventured, nothing gained, right?

Turn to page 152 – there be dragons!

Beef Patties

You'll see these in every Caribbean bakery – they're just like a West Indian version of Cornish Pasties. These make a great party food, so cook a large batch, then freeze and bake whenever you want them.

Heat the oil in a frying pan, add the onion and fry for 5 minutes. Add the garlic, chilli and minced beef, breaking the meat up with a spatula, and fry until the meat has browned all over.

Add the curry powder and fry for a couple of minutes, then add the tomatoes and stock. Cover and simmer for 20 minutes until the meat is tender and most of the liquid is absorbed. Add the spring onions and leave to cool.

For the pastry, put the flour, turmeric, 1 teaspoon of salt and the butter into a food processor and blitz for a few seconds until the mixture forms crumbs. Using a measuring spoon, add 6 tablespoons of ice cold water and blitz again until the pastry forms a ball. Wrap in clingfilm and chill for 10 minutes.

Preheat the oven to 200°C/400°F/Gas Mark 6. Cut the pastry in half and roll out each piece on a sheet of baking parchment. Cut round a small saucer using a knife to get 10 neat rounds. Re-roll the trimmings as needed.

Dollop a generous spoonful of the beef mixture on one half of each pastry round, leaving a 1cm/½ in border around the edge. Brush the edges with water, then fold the pastry over the edges and press down with a fork to seal. Pierce fork holes in the centre of each pattie.

Lift the patties with the baking parchment onto a couple of baking trays. If you want to freeze some, cover a tray with foil and freeze unbaked. Brush the remaining patties with beaten egg to glaze and bake for 25 minutes (or 35 minutes from frozen) until the pastry is golden, the base is firm and the filling is piping hot. When cooking from frozen, don't forget to brush with the egg before putting in the oven.

Makes 10

2 tbsp sunflower oil

1 onion, finely chopped

2 garlic cloves, crushed

1 Scotch bonnet chilli, deseeded and chopped

500g/1lb 2oz beef mince

3 tbsp medium curry powder

225g/8oz can chopped tomatoes

150ml/5fl oz beef stock

2 spring onions, chopped

For the pastry

450g/1lb plain flour, sifted

2 tbsp ground turmeric

salt

225g/8oz butter, chilled and cubed

1 egg, lightly beaten

Special Coleslaw

Coleslaw's the perfect side for a Jamaican barbecue feast. I reckon the sweetcorn and peppers in this one make it supreme.

Put the cabbage into a bowl, add the red and green pepper and mix together.

Stir in the carrots and sweetcorn. Add the mayonnaise, salad cream and black pepper and stir together well.

Serves 8

¼ white cabbage, finely sliced

1 red pepper, cored, deseeded and chopped

1 green pepper, cored, deseeded and chopped

3 large carrots, peeled and grated

298g/10oz can sweetcorn, drained

200ml/7fl oz mayonnaise

100ml/3½fl oz salad cream

2 tsp coarse ground black pepper

Reggae Pizza

Preheat the oven to 240°C/450°F/Gas Mark 9. Put the pizza base mix in a bowl, add 1 tablespoon of the oil and 225ml/8fl oz warm water and mix together to make a soft dough.

Put the tomatoes, garlic, spicy tomato ketchup and oregano in another bowl and mix together, then season with black pepper.

Oil a large baking sheet and roll out the dough on a lightly floured surface to about 30 x 33cm/12 x 13in and lift onto the baking sheet.

Spread the tomato mixture over the dough base and sprinkle with the mozzarella cheese. Arrange the anchovies and black olives on top and drizzle with the rest of the olive oil.

Bake for 20–25 minutes until the base is crisp. Cut into wedges to serve.

TIP: Add some fresh pineapple to give this pizza an authentic Caribbean flavour

Serves 4

290g/10oz packet pizza base mix

4 tbsp olive oil, plus extra for oiling

400g/14oz can chopped tomatoes, drained

2 garlic cloves, crushed

1–2 tbsp spicy tomato ketchup or Love Apple Tomato Sauce

1 tsp dried oregano

freshly ground black pepper

plain flour, for dusting

125g/4½oz mozzarella cheese, drained and diced

50g/2oz can anchovy fillets, drained and cut in half lengthways

50g/2oz pitted black olives

Rasta Pasta

Empty the tomatoes into a pan and add the garlic, spicy tomato ketchup, dried herbs and roasted peppers. Add the sugar and season with salt and black pepper. Cover and heat gently for 10 minutes, then add the olives and turn off the heat.

Meanwhile, bring a large pan of salted water to the boil and cook the spaghetti for 8 minutes, or according to the packet instructions, until it is al dente or tender with a slight bite. Drain the pasta, return to the pan, add the tomato sauce and toss together.

ROOTS RECOMMENDS:
For meat lovers, add a handful of pepperoni to the tomato sauce with the olives..

Serves 4

375g/13oz dried spaghetti

salt and freshly ground black pepper

400g/14oz can cherry tomatoes in tomato sauce

1 garlic clove, finely chopped

2–3 tbsp spicy tomato ketchup or Love Apple Tomato Sauce

1 tsp mixed dried herbs

3 roasted peppers, drained from jar, chopped

pinch of sugar

4 tbsp mixed olives

Levi's Salad

This cool salad goes perfectly with hot island food.

Run a vegetable peeler along the carrots to make carrot shavings.

Arrange the lettuce in a serving dish and fill each lettuce leaf with a selection of the other vegetables and the cashews, if you are using them.

Season with salt and black pepper and drizzle with olive oil. Serve with a dollop of dipping sauce.

'Empty bag can't stan'up'

You can't work on an empty belly

Serves 4

2 carrots, peeled

1 cos lettuce

handful of cherry tomatoes (about 75g/3oz), halved

8 radishes, quartered

1 ripe avocado

1 courgette, sliced

1/2 cucumber, chopped

198g/200g can sweetcorn, drained (optional)

2 spring onions, white part chopped

50g/2oz salted cashew nuts (optional)

salt and freshly ground black pepper

1 tbsp virgin olive oil

sweet chilli dipping sauce or Fiery Guava Dipping Sauce, to serve

No carnival is complete without food straight from the barbecue. Jamaican barbecuing is all about jerk.

Jerk is a style of cooking native to Jamaica. The uncooked meat is dry-rubbed with a spicy mixture known as Jamaican Jerk and then grilled on a barbecue. Traditionally, pork was used but now it's often chicken and fish. Jerk spice can include many ingredients, such as cinnamon, garlic, cloves and nutmeg, but it must contain two key flavours to get the right level of spice: Jamaican pimento (otherwise known as allspice) and Scotch bonnet peppers, which really give it that kick!

The traditional Jamaican way to barbecue is to use an old oil drum that's been cut in half. Not got one of those? Then go for any barbecue with a lid to keep the smoky flavour locked in.

The type of wood or charcoal you use will determine the ultimate flavour of the food. The traditional jerk wood is pimento wood or hickory, and the smoke created gives the food its distinctive flavour. Look out for hickory wooden chips in shops to throw on with the charcoal.

Levi's Juicy Jerk Seasoning

Makes enough to serve 4

Here's how to give your food a Jamaican flavour to savour. You can buy jerk seasoning in the shops, but this is the real deal.

Put the chillies, spring onion, onion, allspice, ginger, garlic, herbs, all-purpose seasoning, nutmeg and cinnamon into a food processor and whiz until smooth. Mix in the coriander leaves, salt, black pepper and tomato ketchup.

Store in an airtight container or a small screwtop jar in the refrigerator for up to 2 weeks.

4 Scotch bonnet chillies, deseeded and chopped

1 spring onion, green end only, chopped

1 onion, chopped

2 tbsp ground allspice (pimento)

2.5cm/1in piece fresh root ginger, peeled and grated

2 garlic cloves, crushed

3 tbsp mixed dried herbs

1 tbsp dried basil

3 tbsp all-purpose seasoning

1 tsp fresh ground nutmeg

1 tsp ground cinnamon

2 tbsp fresh coriander leaves

1 tsp salt

2 tbsp coarse ground black pepper

500ml/18fl oz bottle tomato ketchup

Levi's Dry Jerk Seasoning

Put the all-purpose seasoning, ground allspice, mixed herbs, salt and pepper in a bowl and mix together.

Store in an airtight container for up to 1 month.

Makes enough to serve 4

1 tsp all-purpose seasoning

1 tsp ground allspice

1 tsp mixed dried savory, marjoram, oregano, thyme, rosemary, basil and tarragon

1 tsp salt

1 tsp ground black pepper

Jerk Chicken

This Jerk recipe is generations old, passed down to me by my grandmother and it has remained a family secret... until now!

Rinse the chicken under cold running water, then sprinkle over the lemon juice, drain and pat dry with kitchen paper.

Put the chicken into a non-metallic dish. Rub in the dry seasoning, then pour on Levi's Juicy Jerk Seasoning and turn the chicken until coated. Chill for 4 hours or overnight, if you've time.

Get your barbecue red-hot. Put the chicken on the barbecue, cover and cook for 10 minutes on each side or until the juices run clear when you push a knife into the centre.

When the chicken's thoroughly cooked, transfer to a chopping board and chop each piece into about 4 portions with the bones. Serve with chilli barbecue sauce.

Serves 8

8 chicken quarters with skin

juice of 1 lemon

1 quantity Levi's Dry Jerk Seasoning (see above)

1 quantity Levi's Juicy Jerk Seasoning (see page 131)

chilli barbecue sauce or Reggae Reggae Sauce, to serve

'When chicken tie up chicken, cockroach want explanation.

You suspect a trick or things aren't how they appear

Jerk Roast Snapper

Rinse the fish inside and out under cold running water and pat dry with kitchen paper. Cut a few slashes into each side of the fish with a sharp knife.

Put the all-purpose seasoning, allspice, mixed dried herbs, salt and black pepper into a bowl and mix together, then rub into the fish flesh.

Push the thyme and spring onions inside the cavity of each fish.

Heat the barbecue. Lightly coat 4 sheets of foil with a little of the oil and put a fish on top of each piece. Wrap each fish securely in the foil and put on top of the barbecue. Cook for 20 minutes.

Serve with sweet chilli or Fiery Guava dipping sauce.

Serves 4

4 red snapper, scaled, gutted and cleaned

1 tsp all-purpose seasoning

1 tsp ground allspice (pimento)

1 tsp mixed dried savory, marjoram, oregano, thyme, rosemary, basil and tarragon (Herbes de Provence)

1 tsp salt

1 tsp ground black pepper

4 fresh thyme sprigs

4 spring onions, chopped

2 tbsp olive oil

sweet chilli dipping sauce or Fiery Guava Dipping Sauce, to serve

Jerk Lamb

Rinse the lamb under cold running water, then sprinkle over the lemon juice, drain and pat dry with kitchen paper.

Put the lamb in a non-metallic dish and rub in the dry seasoning, then pour on Levi's Juicy Jerk Seasoning and turn the lamb until coated. Chill for 4 hours or overnight, if you've time.

Heat the barbecue. Put the lamb on the barbecue, cover and cook for 10 minutes on each side or until the meat is cooked.

When the lamb's thoroughly cooked, transfer to a chopping board and chop each piece into about 4 portions with the bones.

Serve with sweet chilli dipping sauce.

Serves 4

8 best end of neck cutlets

juice of 1 lemon

1 quantity Levi's Dry Jerk Seasoning (see page 132)

1 quantity Levi's Juicy Jerk Seasoning (see page 131)

sweet chilli dipping sauce or Fiery Guava Dipping Sauce, to serve

Barbecued Escovitch Prawns

Shrimps, prawns, whatever you want to call them – these are the business – eaten warm from the coals and pepped up with a vinegary twang. Get stuck in with some bread for a real easy treat.

Sprinkle the prawns with the lemon juice, then pierce the shell in several places. This helps the seasoning flavours to penetrate the flesh.

Put the all-purpose seasoning, allspice, mixed dried herbs, salt and black pepper in a bowl and mix together, then rub into the prawns.

Get your barbecue nice and hot and then throw on the prawns. Cook for a few minutes until they turn pink. You could also cook them on a hot grill pan.

While the prawns are cooking, heat the oil in a pan, add the onion, pepper, spring onions and vinegar and heat until warmed through.

Put the prawns onto a serving plate and pour over the vegetables and vinegar to serve.

Serves 4

8 raw king prawns, in shells

juice of 1 lemon

1 tsp all-purpose seasoning

1 tsp ground allspice (pimento)

1 tsp mixed dried savory, marjoram, oregano, thyme, rosemary, basil and tarragon

1 tsp salt

1 tsp ground black pepper

2 tsp vegetable oil

1 onion, sliced

½ green pepper, deseeded and sliced

2 spring onions, green ends only, chopped

2 tbsp malt vinegar

ROOTS RECOMMENDS:
The combination of dried savory, marjoram, oregano, thyme, rosemary, basil and tarragon is often called Herbes de Provence and is widely available in supermarkets.

Reggae Reggae Kebab

Pierce the chicken flesh several times, sprinkle over the lemon juice and season generously with salt and black pepper.

Add the Reggae Reggae sauce or any chilli barbecue sauce, and stir well to mix. Cover and leave to marinate in the refrigerator for 4 hours or overnight, if you've time.

Soak 4 wooden skewers in a large bowl of water for at least 30 minutes. This will help them not to burn.

Brush off some of the sauce from the chicken, then thread alternate pieces of chicken, green pepper, red pepper and pineapple pieces onto the soaked wooden skewers.

Heat the barbecue and cook the skewers for 15 minutes, turning regularly until the chicken is cooked through and tender.

Serves 4

4 skinless, boneless chicken breasts, cut into cubes

juice of 1/2 lemon

salt and coarse ground black pepper

8 tbsp chilli barbecue sauce or Reggae Reggae Sauce

1 green pepper, cored, deseeded and cut into cubes

1 red pepper, cored, deseeded and cut into cubes

1 fresh pineapple slice, peeled and cut into 4 pieces

'Cubbitch fe one plantain yuh lose the whole bunch'

Give a little or you might just lose the whole lot

Barbecue Extras

Baked Plantain

Cut off the top and bottom of the plantain, then cut a slit down one side. Cut in half, wrap in foil and place on a hot barbecue for 30 minutes, turning occasionally.

Unwrap the foil, peel the plantain and serve.

Serves 2

1 plantain, topped, tailed and a slit cut down one side

Roast Yam

Heat the barbecue. Brush the yam with the oil and put directly onto the barbecue. Cook for about 20 minutes, turning constantly, until the yam is tender and browned.

Serve with Roast Saltfish (see below).

Serves 2

1 large yam, peeled
2 tsp olive oil

Roast Saltfish

Heat the barbecue. Scrape the excess salt off the fish with a knife and put the block of salted cod directly onto the barbecue. Cook, turning constantly, until crispy.

Coat with the spicy tomato sauce and serve with Roast Yam (see above).

Serves 2

225g/8oz block salted cod

spicy tomato ketchup or Love Apple Tomato Sauce, to serve

Roast Corn on the Cob

If you're up against the clock, you can cook raw cobs straight on the barbecue without boiling them first. Just brush with oil or give them a quick soak in water. Whilst the corn is cooking, remember to keep turning it.

Heat the barbecue. Put the corn onto the barbecue and cook for 10 minutes, turning as needed, until the corn is tender.

Peel away the husk and season with salt and add a knob of butter.

Serves 4

4 corn on the cobs with outer husks intact

salt

4 knobs of butter

Roasted Breadfruit

Breadfruit is a staple food of many tropical regions. It is cooked and served in a very similar way to potato.

Cut out the stem from the breadfruit and place stem-side down over a barbecue. Turn until evenly charred all over. It is ready when the whole breadfruit is blackened on the outside and a knife can be easily pushed into the fruit.

Allow to cool slightly, then peel off the charred skin with a knife. Cut into thick wedges and serve topped with a knob of butter.

Makes 16 wedges

1 semi-ripe breadfruit

25g/1oz butter

'Ole fire–stick easy fe ketch'

It's easy for old acquaintances to make up

Guinness Punch

My special Irish-Caribbean punch is great for a party!

Pour the Guinness into a large jug, add the condensed milk, evaporated milk, vanilla essence, Caribbean essence and nutmeg. Chill and serve over ice.

Serves 6

1 litre/1³/₄ pints Guinness

400g/14oz can sweetened condensed milk

175g/6oz evaporated milk

¹/₂ tsp vanilla essence

¹/₂ tsp mixed Caribbean essence

pinch of ground nutmeg

crushed ice, to serve

Pineapple Punch

Pour the pineapple juice into a large jug, add the condensed milk, evaporated milk, vanilla essence, Angostura bitters, Caribbean essence and nutmeg.

Chill and serve over ice.

Serves 6

1 litre/1³/₄ pints pineapple juice

400g/14oz can sweetened condensed milk

dash of Angostura bitters

175g/6oz evaporated milk

¹/₂ tsp vanilla essence

¹/₂ tsp mixed Caribbean essence

pinch of ground nutmeg

crushed ice, to serve

Ginger Beer

This 'beer' will give you a kick, but not a hangover!

Put the ginger, orange peel, lemon juice and sugar into a large pan and pour on 3 litres/5¼ pints boiling water. Cover and leave overnight.

Strain the liquid into a large jug and add the Angostura bitters.

Pour into 3 bottles, add a clove to each bottle, seal and leave in a warm place for 3–4 days. Serve with ice.

Serves 6

125g/4½oz piece fresh root ginger, peeled and grated

peel of 1 orange

1 tbsp lemon juice

1kg/2lb 4oz golden caster sugar

dash of Angostura bitters

3 cloves

ice, to serve

Rum Punch

This recipe makes a lot, so it is just right for a party.

Put the sugar into a large jug, pour on 8 tablespoons of boiling water and stir until the sugar has dissolved .

Add the lime juice, rum and Angostura bitters, then chill for a couple of hours.

To serve, add the citrus fruit slices, ice and top up with lemonade to taste, if you like.

Serves 10

100g/3½oz golden caster sugar

125ml/4½fl oz lime juice

75cl/26fl oz bottle white or dark rum

few drops of Angostura bitters

To serve

1 lemon, cut into slices

1 lime, cut into slices

1 orange, cut into slices

ice

1 litre/1¾ pints bottle lemonade (optional)

Frozen Mango Daiquiri

Guaranteed to make you feel like you're on holiday!

Put the mango juice, rum, lime juice, sugar and ice into
a blender and whiz together until thick and slushy.

Serve in a cocktail glass.

Serves 4

400ml/14fl oz mango juice

200ml/8fl oz white rum

100ml/4fl oz lime juice

4 tsp golden caster sugar

4 glassfuls of crushed ice
(about 600ml/1 pint)

Punch of Crema

This is a popular Christmas drink but delicious at
any time of year.

Put the eggs, evaporated milk, condensed milk, rum,
vanilla essence, Angostura bitters, nutmeg and lemon zest
into a large bowl and whisk to combine. Add sugar to taste.

Drink straightaway or pour into a bottle and store in the
refrigerator for up to 3 days.

Serves 6

6 eggs

400g/14oz can evaporated milk

400g/14oz can sweetened
condensed milk

300ml/10fl oz dark rum

$\frac{1}{2}$ tsp vanilla essence

2 tsp Angostura bitters

pinch of freshly grated nutmeg

finely grated zest of 1 lemon

golden caster sugar, to taste

'When yuh neighbour beard catch
fire, tek water wet fe yuh'

Learn from others' mistakes

Sorrel

This is a Jamaican drink traditionally drunk at Christmas. Look out for dried sorrel in Asian and Caribbean food stores in December.

Using a vegetable peeler, peel away a large strip of orange zest and put it into a large jug with the sorrel, cinnamon stick, cloves and ginger.

Add the sugar and pour on 1.7 litres/3 pints boiling water, then stir to dissolve. Cover and leave overnight.

Strain, chill and serve over crushed ice.

Serves 6

1 orange

25g/1oz dried sorrel

7.5cm/3in cinnamon stick

5 cloves

1cm/½in piece fresh root ginger, peeled and grated

450g/1lb golden caster sugar

crushed ice, to serve

Licka Watermelon

A big, impressive carnival treat! It's easy to make but you'll need to start it a few days before your party. Make sure it's well chilled.

Cut a hole in the top of the watermelon which is wide and deep enough to squeeze a funnel into. Pour some vodka or rum into the melon (it'll only take so much) and leave to chill for a day in the refrigerator.

Repeat this over a few days, about 3, until the watermelon is saturated with the vodka.

Slice and serve!

Serves 20

1 large ripe watermelon

vodka or white rum (use as much as you need)

Cheat's Pina Colada Granita

Put the rum, coconut cream, double cream, sugar, pineapple juice and crushed ice into a blender.

Whiz everything together and pour into 2 cocktail glasses.

Halve the pineapple slices, and cut a slit in each slice, put on the edge of the glasses to decorate.

Serves 4

200ml/7fl oz white rum

100ml/4fl oz coconut cream

100ml/4fl oz double cream

4 tbsp golden caster sugar

300ml/½ pint pineapple juice

600ml/1 pint crushed ice

4 fresh pineapple slices,
to decorate

Mojito

Put the mint, lime and sugar into a tumbler glass and mash together with a spoon.

Pour on the rum, add the ice cubes and top up with soda water.

Serves 4

4 fresh mint sprig

8 lime wedges

8 tsp golden caster sugar

200ml/8fl oz white rum

lots of ice cubes

soda water, to serve

SLAYING THE DRAGONS

When I quit my driving job, I threw myself into turning my food into a business. In some ways, I was going into it blind: all that I had to cling to for encouragement was the knowledge that thousands of people at Carnival loved my food and came back for more year after year.

I needed to think of a name for my grandmother's sauce, find a firm to supply me with bottles, and work out a business plan. I knew nothing about computers so I enrolled on a course and studied hard. Within a few weeks, all the money I'd saved from driving had gone.

Initially I couldn't decide on a name for the sauce. I thought of calling it something conventional such as King's Hot Pepper Sauce. It would have been a safe bet, but instinctively I wanted the name to reflect what I am about, which is music, and food, and fun.

Then it came to me: Reggae Reggae Sauce! It might be a mouthful (pun intended) but it is true to me and because it is special and slightly quirky and silly, it is memorable. Before I knew it, I had designed the label with my new hard-earned computer skills and even written the special Reggae Reggae Sauce song:

♪♪ Put some music in my food for me
Gimme some reggae reggae sauce
Hot reggae reggae sauce
It's so nice I had to name it twice
I called it reggae reggae sauce
Hot reggae reggae sauce

Just like my baby it's the perfect delight
It's got some peppers and some herbs
and spice
We want some reggae reggae sauce
Hot reggae reggae sauce

So nice with your fried chicken
Makes burgers finger-licking
On rice and peas and fish
Put some reggae sauce on your lips ♪

Everything was looking good – except that I was skint. I had spent all my money on bottles, labels and posters and five months in college and I needed help. So I visited all the banks trying to secure financial backing and got… nowhere. They liked my business plan, but the problem with banks is you have to have money before they'll lend you money!

Then I got lucky. I met another of these occasional mentors who light my way. A woman called Nadia Jones at Greater London Enterprise (GLE1), got me a £1,000 start-up loan. I didn't get the money straight away, but it was a big encouragement.

Meanwhile, we were cooking up a reggae reggae storm in the kitchen at home in Brixton all summer long. We just had the one battered old pot that made enough sauce to fill 65 bottles at a time – and our set target for the Carnival was 4,000 bottles. Let me tell you, there was a lot of cooking going on!

That year's Carnival was beyond my wildest dreams. We sold out of all 4,000 bottles of Reggae Reggae Sauce, and it wasn't just punters buying it: it was all the other stallholders, because at last they could make their food taste as good as ours! My last doubts and reservations fell away: I knew I was on to something big.

There was still a lot to do. Outside of Carnival, the only places selling the sauce were Brixton Market and a local CD shop called Red's Records, who sold more sauce than they did CDs! Nadia Jones had pointed me towards going to trade fairs to get the name better known, so in November I fetched up at the World Food Market in Docklands.

In my experience those trade shows can be as quiet as the grave, so I decided to jazz up the place with some music. Getting out my ghetto blaster, I turned up some Bob Marley, and before you knew it, the Caribbean corner of the exhibition was rammed with people coming to see what all the fuss was about.

Retailers and distributors asked to taste the sauce and loved it, and in no time I had more than 300 business cards in my pockets. Then a woman came over to talk to me. She said she was from Dragon's Den and that she thought I'd be great for the show and she'd like me to audition. I looked at this woman and thought to myself: 'What the hell is Dragon's Den?' It didn't sound like something a Rasta man would get involved with!

She told me it was a TV programme, a reality show, and I thought about 'I'm A Celebrity... Get Me Out Of Here!' and imagined she wanted to have me eating bugs or have snakes crawling over me! She laughed, and explained the idea of the show and I said, 'OK, I will ask my kids and see what they think.'

My kids knew the show but didn't think it was a good idea to go on it. They told me, 'Dad, you're a black guy from Brixton with four-foot dreadlocks – you are going to take your business plan to all those clean-cut business guys?' They said I would get ripped to pieces. Luckily, I don't have to listen to my kids – they have to listen to me! I listen to my mother.

So, I went to my mother and told her the scenario of the show. She has great faith in me, so she told me to believe in myself and in what I do. She is a great Christian and relies heavily on her Bible, and she told me to read Psalm 23:

The Lord is my shepherd; I shall not want
He makes me to lie down in green pastures;
he leads me besides the still waters.
He restores my soul.

She told me to concentrate on 'I shall not want…' and told me that if I went to our Maker and said, 'I don't want to be wanting any more', I would become a Dragon-slayer. That was enough for me. I decided that I would enter the fearsome creatures' lair.

I had to go to an audition shortly before Christmas. The Dragons were not in their Den but let me tell you, it was still a daunting experience. I took my guitar and sang the Reggae Reggae Sauce song and even put in a new line for them:

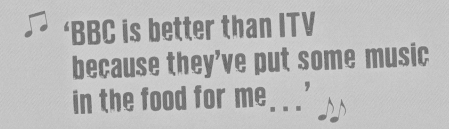

'BBC is better than ITV because they've put some music in the food for me…'

The producers loved that. They made me talk to camera and asked me 45 minutes of questions about who I am and what I'm all about, then at the end of it all, they said: 'You're in – you're doing the show!'

So the day dawned. Tuesday 9 January 2007; the day I slew the Dragons, like a modern take on Daniel in the lions' den, Jason slaying the Hydra or Maximus and the Gladiators. It was a famous day that changed my life – but it didn't get off to a very good start.

I was broke. I had £20 in my pocket; all I had to my name. The mini-cab controller said it would cost £12 to take me to the Dragons' Den in London Bridge. I thought of taking the bus but I had too much equipment to carry. How would I get home? I didn't even know if they would feed me.

When we got there I gave the cabbie £10. He took it without saying a word and sped away quickly, leaving me standing in the cold. It was 6a.m. and I was one hour ahead of everybody else, full of life and raring to go.

Before I had left home I had read Psalms 23 as my mother had told me to. I was dressed immaculately in a crisp black suit, chalk white shirt, black-and-white polka dot tie and waist coat decked off with seven large golden buttons, Italian shoes and a Coco Chanel diamond bling belt. It was show time.

I had decided to ask the Dragons for £50,000 for 20 per cent of my business. By now, I knew what I had to do: pitch, barter and sell my business to five multi-millionaires. If I could convince them I could make them a fantastic return if they invested in my t'ing, I would get the money.

Inside the studio, my rival contestants paced up and down. They were all at fever pitch. David, a likeable Essex man in his late 60s, was muttering to himself and clutching what looked like a thousand-page business plan. He had a whole range of perfumes he had developed, that he thought would knock these ferocious ogres out cold. He looked nervous.

John had invented a horsewhip with a wing mirror on the end so the jockey could see who was coming up behind him! I thought it was rubbish – I couldn't see Frankie Dettori rushing out to buy one.! I shook my head and thought, 'Those beasts will have a feast with him.'

A young guy called William showed me his contraption that dried clothes outside in the rain. It was clever, but he seemed to have no confidence in his product. Beverley, a young designer from Dulwich, was talking herself through her business plan and seemed in a right state. I could tell there would be tears before the day was out for a lot of people.

I was the only black guy there and people were giving me some weird looks. I could see them thinking: 'This Rasta man who is pretending to be Bob Marley – why isn't he panicking? What's so cool about his pitch?' But my ignorance was working in my favour. I had never seen the show, and you can't fear something if you're not aware of it!

It was time for me to check my equipment: load up my ammo. My secret weapon to slay the Dragons was playing my guitar and singing the Reggae Reggae Sauce song. I picked it up and started to tune up, but disaster struck! The G string busted... THWACK!!!

The sound vibrated around the room like a pistol shot. Everyone looked on gobsmacked and an eerie silence descended. Of course, I hadn't bought a replacement with me! Anger and panic began to set in. I fiddled with the tuning, and THWACK!!! Another one, this time the A string! Jah, what is happening to me? Not now!

A member of the film crew, Michelle, volunteered to go and get strings for me seven miles away in Kennington. She knew that without my guitar I didn't stand a chance. The Dragons would make jerk chicken out of me, and my efforts would be wasted. I needed my guitar fixed, NOW!

The two hours Michelle was gone seemed to last an eternity but then she returned to cheers from all the crew. I carefully restrung, slowly, tightening, turning… THWACK!!! No! Not again! It busted again – would you Adam and Eve it?

At this point, I gave up. What will be will be. Not only did I only have five strings but in my desperation I had damaged the guitar's tuning keys, so I couldn't even retune it. Defeated, I leant it up against the wall and told the production crew that I wanted to go home. The day was doomed.

Michelle begged me to try again. They were all desperate for me to appear. Eventually I reluctantly agreed to have one last go. I picked my stricken guitar from where it was standing uselessly against the wall and gently strummed it. I knew it was going to sound horrible…

But what was this? Miraculously, it sounded fine. I held down G minor and that sounded OK too. I didn't know what to say. Was this a miracle? Nobody had touched it, that's for sure! So I placed it back, carefully, in the same place up against the wall and watched it closely for the next four hours. I wasn't going to have my secret weapon taken away again.

So finally it was my turn to go upstairs and face down the Dragons. There was only me and one other bloke left: there had been no winners all day. The Dragons had chewed them all up and spat them out. But I was feeling good. I had my weapon back, and this was what I know: Performance.

It was showtime. I walked up the stairs, strumming my guitar and singing my song...

♪♪ **Put some music in my food for me**
Gimme some reggae reggae sauce
Hot reggae reggae sauce
It's so nice I had to name it twice ♫

It was pitch black in the Den except for a giant spotlight smack in the middle of the floor, like on Mastermind. Then I saw the five Dragons; dressed immaculately in black, slouching in their leather executive chairs. They had in front of them on small tables the treasures I was here for; huge piles of £50 notes, stacked up high.

The magic spell had worked and my guitar sounded great now, like a top-of-the-range Gibson 12-string. The tuning disaster was a distant memory. I could see the Dragons loved the Reggae Reggae Sauce song: they were smiling and even tapping their toes (or should I say claws and talons?).

First blood to me, then. When I started talking, I made a mistake in my presentation, saying I already had an order for 2.5 million litres of the sauce rather than 500 litres, but I managed to recover quickly. Then it was time to deliver my killer blow: feeding the Dragons my Reggae Reggae Sauce.

That morning in my kitchen, I had prepared a beautiful little china bowl filled with tasty morsels of chicken, celery and pieces of cheese skewered on tiny dipsticks. There were two flavours of Reggae Reggae Sauce, mild and hot, but I had made sure I had used the mild one… hadn't I?

The Dragons all dived in, except for Duncan Bannatyne, who said that he didn't like sauces or spicy foods. I quipped to him: 'What a Dragon! No fire on your breath, then?' He smiled back… but what was happening with the other Dragons?

'Ahh! Ahh!' One of them was shouting loudly while vigorously fanning his mouth in a frenzy. Tears trickled from his eyes. The female Dragon, Deborah, exclaimed: 'Wow, this is so hot!' She looked ashen and pale: the ferocious Scotch-bonnet peppers had attacked the poor woman's tongue without warning.

The third Dragon was clawing for a glass of water, downing it in one and staring at me through bloodshot eyes. They were all spluttering. My heart skipped several beats as I realized the awful truth: I had picked up the hot samples by mistake! I'd blown it! Damn, who had switched the bottles?

I was sure the Dragons were about to 'Nyam me up and fill dem craw' – but what was this? The fifth Dragon, Peter Jones, was licking his lips while dunking and smothering a cheese morsel in Reggae Reggae Sauce. He loved it: 'Him nyam off the whole plate, and ready fi lick out the bowl tu…!'

Phew! I had survived my mistake – but that didn't mean the Dragons were on my side. Duncan said he liked my presentation but didn't think the market was there for the sauce. Theo said he thought I didn't need external investment. Deborah just said it wasn't for her. Suddenly there were only two Dragons left.

Peter Jones looked me up and down. 'I like you Levi, and I think the sauce is great too,' he said. He told me he wouldn't buy Reggae Reggae Sauce if it wasn't me selling it to him, he praised my dress sense and presentation, and then he pounced: he would offer £25,000 – half of my asking price – for a full 20 per cent of my business. This Dragon had got me in a corner, trapped.

I still needed Richard, the last Dragon, on board or I would get nothing. The show's rules were very clear; you had to get the minimum of your original asking price from one or more of the Dragons. Richard had enjoyed the singing during my pitch and now he was interested in a deal as well. So I knew what was coming: Richard would join the battle too but he was going to want the same deal as his partner-in-crime.

Richard did exactly as I thought; he wanted in, but like his rival Peter, he too wanted 20 per cent for £25,000 of investment. I had some serious thinking to do on the spot, and quick.

So, what was it to be? I could walk away as a winner on national TV with £50,000 in my bank account, two multi-millionaires as my partners in Reggae Reggae Sauce and £500,000 worth of free advertising… or I could stick to my guns, refuse it all and go home broke. What a dilemma! What am I to do? Well I accepted of course! After having a chat with the presenter, Evan Davies, I got a taxi.

'Where to, mate'? The taxi-driver asked me as he looked through his rear view mirror. 'Brixton' I said. My mobile phone had been switched off all day so I powered up and dialled… 'Hello Mum, I've done it! I slayed dem Dragons!'

So then what happened? Read on, page 184.

SWEET SATISFACTION

Give yourself a treat with these Caribbean sweets.

Mango Sorbet

This sorbet leaves a nice clean taste on your tongue.

Put the sugar and 600ml/1 pint water into a pan and heat gently until the sugar dissolves, then increase the heat and boil for 5 minutes. Leave to cool.

Peel the mangoes, cut the flesh away from the stone and put into a blender. Whiz together to make a smooth purée. You should have about 600ml/1 pint of mango flesh.

Put the mango flesh, sugar syrup and lime juice in a large bowl and mix together. Transfer to an ice-cream maker and churn to make a smooth sorbet.

Alternatively, pour the mixture into a large plastic freezerproof container and freeze for 1 hour. Remove from the freezer, transfer to the blender and whiz to break up the ice crystals. Return the mixture to the container and freeze for another couple of hours.

ROOTS RECOMMENDS:
If you can't find good value mangoes,
use 2 x 400g/14oz canned mangoes instead.

Serves 4–6

250g/9oz golden caster sugar
4 large juicy mangoes
juice of 1 lime

'If a man can't dance
im say de music no good'

Tropical Fruit Salad

Refreshing and healthy!

Serves 6

Put the watermelon, mango, papaya, pineapple and oranges into a large bowl and mix together. Scoop out the pulp and seeds from the passion fruit and add to the other fruit. Chill until needed.

¼–½ watermelon, depending if large, flesh removed from skin and cubed

1 mango, peeled, flesh removed from the stone and sliced

1 papaya, peeled, halved, deseeded and sliced

½ fresh pineapple, peeled, cored and cubed

2 oranges, peeled, white pith removed and sliced

2 passion fruit, halved

Papaya and Lime

This is a super-fast and refreshing treat. Choose a ripe papaya that gives a little when gently squeezed.

Serves 2

Cut away the peel with a sharp knife, then cut the papaya in half. Use a spoon to scoop out the black seeds and throw them away.

1 papaya
1 lime, halved

Cut the papaya into wedges, put on to a couple of plates and squeeze over the lime juice to serve.

Grilled Spiced Pineapple

You can tell if a pineapple is ripe and ready to eat by pulling on one of the green spiky leaves. If they come out really easily, then the pineapple is ripe.

Preheat the grill. Cut the top and base off the pineapple, reserving the top leaves for the decoration.

Cut into 6 wedges, then slice the tough woody core away from the centre of each piece. Cut the flesh away from the skin on each pineapple wedge. Slice each piece across several times to make little slices.

Put the pineapple on to a baking tray and sprinkle each piece with the mixed spice, Angostura bitters and brown sugar.

Cook under the hot grill for a few minutes until the pineapple flesh is warmed through and the sugar has melted.

Serves 6

1 whole fresh pineapple

1 tsp ground mixed spice

splash of Angostura bitters

2 tbsp soft brown or molasses sugar

Hot Sugar Cane Bananas

The dark sugar gives these bananas a really wonderful caramel flavour.

Make a slit down the length of the bananas, without cutting right through. Open the skin slightly and dot the bananas with the butter and sprinkle each one with the sugar.

Put the bananas into a shallow dish and microwave on high for 3–4 minutes until the skins turn black and the banana flesh is warm and soft.

Serves 4

4 ripe bananas
knob of butter
4 tsp dark muscovado sugar

ROOTS RECOMMENDS:
Haven't got a microwave? Then bake them in a pre-heated oven at 190°C/375°F/Gas Mark 5 for 15 minutes.

Coconut Cake

This simple cake is the business!

Preheat the oven to 180°C/350°F/Gas Mark 4 and line a 900g/2lb loaf tin with non-stick baking parchment.

Put the flour, baking powder, butter, sugar, eggs, coconut and lime zest and juice into a large bowl and mix together with an electric whisk. Start off slowly, then gradually increase the speed. If you haven't got a mixer, put all the ingredients into a large bowl and mix together with a wooden spoon until light and fluffy.

Pour the mixture into the prepared tin and bake for 45–55 minutes or until a skewer inserted into the centre comes out clean. Leave to cool in the tin for 10 minutes, then turn on to a wire rack to cool completely.

Serves 12

175g/6oz self-raising flour

1 tsp baking powder

175g/6oz butter, cut into cubes

175g/6oz golden caster sugar

3 eggs, lightly beaten

50g/2oz sweetened tenderised coconut or desiccated coconut

finely grated zest and juice of 2 limes

'When fire deh a mus-mus tail im think a cool breeze'

Some people never recognise danger

Easy Coconut Ice Cream

Put the cream in a large bowl and whip until softly peaking, then add the coconut. Stir in the condensed milk, custard, vanilla essence, Caribbean essence and ground nutmeg.

Line a 900g/2lb loaf tin with clingfilm. Pour in the coconut mixture and freeze for 6 hours.

To serve, scoop into balls or invert onto a plate, remove the clingfilm and slice into 6 pieces.

Serves 6

300ml/10fl oz double cream

125g/4¹/₂oz sweetened tenderised coconut or desiccated coconut or grated fresh coconut

200g/7oz can sweetened condensed milk

200g/7oz carton fresh custard

1 tbsp vanilla essence

2 tsp mixed Caribbean essence

pinch of ground nutmeg

Fast Banana Ice Cream

Got any bananas that are looking a little past it? Whack them in the freezer, and when you've an urge for ice cream just whiz them up in a processor with natural yogurt and get stuck in straight away.

Put the sliced bananas on to a large non-stick tray and freeze for 30 minutes.

Put the frozen bananas into a food processor with 1 tablespoon of natural yogurt, the orange juice and vanilla essence. Whiz together until smooth, then add the remaining natural yogurt, if needed to make it creamy. Serve straight away.

Serves 4–6

6 ripe bananas, about 700g/ 1lb 9oz, peeled and sliced

2 tbsp natural yogurt

2 tbsp orange juice

1 tsp vanilla essence

West Indian Christmas Cake

Santa would definitely approve of this yummy fruit cake! Start soaking the fruit in the rum in good time – weeks or even months ahead is best to make it wet and wonderful.

Put the dried fruit and lemon zest into a large jar, pour on the rum and stir everything together. Seal and leave the fruit to macerate for as long as you've got!

Preheat the oven to 180°C/350°F/Gas Mark 4. Grease and line the base and sides of a 20cm/8in cake tin.

Put the butter, sugar and vanilla essence into a large bowl and beat together with a hand-held mixer until light and fluffy. Gradually add the eggs, a little at a time, adding two tablespoons of flour to stop the mixture curdling. Sift the remaining flour, the mixed spice and allspice together, then gently fold into the mixture.

Put half the macerated fruit into a food processor and whiz until it's smooth. Fold into the cake mixture with the rest of the fruit and the rum.

Spoon the mixture into the prepared tin, smoothing over the surface and leaving a slight dip on the surface.

Bake for 1¼ hours or until a cocktail stick or skewer inserted into the centre comes out clean. If it doesn't, bake the cake for a further 15 minutes and check again. Pour over the brandy and leave to cool in the tin.

Turn the cake out of the tin and keep wrapped in foil.

Serves 16

250g/9oz mixed dried fruit

finely grated zest of 1 lemon

300ml/10fl oz dark rum

250g/9oz butter, cut into cubes, plus extra for greasing

225g/8oz molasses sugar

½ tsp vanilla essence

3 medium eggs, lightly beaten

250g/9oz self-raising brown flour

1 tbsp ground mixed spice

½ tsp ground allspice (pimento)

4 tbsp brandy, to finish

'Yuh tan deh call, yuh wud a never get come'

Don't ignore good advice

Banana Cake

This cake is great for using up over-ripe bananas.

Preheat the oven to 180°C/350°F/Gas Mark 4. Grease and base line a 900g/2lb loaf tin with butter.

Sift the flour, bicarbonate of soda and cream of tartar into a food processor, add the butter and sugar and whiz until crumbs form.

Add the lemon juice, milk, banana, eggs and vanilla essence and whiz together to combine.

Spoon the mixture into the prepared tin and bake for 1–1¼ hours or until the cake is risen, golden and a skewer inserted into the centre comes out clean. Leave to cool.

Serves 10

100g/3½oz butter, cut into cubes, plus extra for greasing

225g/8oz plain flour

1 tsp bicarbonate of soda

½ tsp cream of tartar

175g/6oz soft light brown sugar

1 tsp lemon juice

3 tbsp milk

2 bananas, (about 300g/10½oz) peeled and cut into 4 pieces

2 eggs, lightly beaten

1 tsp vanilla essence

'The more yuh chop breadfruit root de more im spring'

The more you fight me,
the more I will fight back

SLOW
BANANA CROSSING
200 FEET AHEAD

Jamaican Bun

This is a sweet bread that's bursting with spicy intrigue. It is made with dark muscovado and treacly molasses sugar to give the cake that delicious rich flavour. Try it with cheese.

Put both flours, the yeast, both sugars, the mixed spice, cinnamon, nutmeg, allspice, salt and vanilla essence into a large bowl.

Warm the butter and milk until just tepid in a small pan. Add to the dry ingredients with the egg, and using your hands, bring the mixture together.

Knead on a lightly floured surface for 10 minutes until smooth and elastic, then cover with greased clingfilm and leave in a warm place.

Lightly grease a baking tray with butter. Empty out the risen dough on to a lightly floured surface, tip in the dried fruit and knead the dough together. Shape into a round and put on to the prepared tray. Cover with greased clingfilm and leave in a warm place for about 1–1½ hours or until the loaf has doubled in size.

Preheat the oven to 190°C/375°F/Gas Mark 5. Bake the bun for 50 minutes until risen and brown.

For the glaze, put the sugar and 3 tablespoons of boiling water in a heatproof bowl and microwave on High for 30 seconds to dissolve the sugar. Alternatively, heat the sugar and water in a small pan until the sugar has dissolved. Brush the glaze over the warm loaf and serve warm, sliced as it is or with a smothering of butter.

Makes 1 large loaf.
Cuts into 10 slices

400g/14oz very strong white flour, plus extra for dusting

100g/3½oz strong brown bread flour

7g/¼oz sachet easy blend dried yeast

75g/3oz dark muscovado sugar

50g/2oz molasses sugar or dark muscovado

1 tsp ground mixed spice

½ tsp ground cinnamon

½ tsp ground nutmeg

½ tsp ground allspice (pimento)

1 tsp salt

1 tsp vanilla essence

100g/3½oz butter, melted, plus extra for greasing

150ml/5fl oz milk

1 egg, lightly beaten

50g/2oz dried mixed fruit

2 tbsp light muscovado sugar, to glaze

butter, to serve (optional)

Jamaican Ginger Cake

This cake is usually made in a loaf tin, but I reckon it's cool in a ring tin too.

Preheat the oven to 150°C/300°F/Gas Mark 2. Grease a 20cm/8in ring tin or a 900g/2lb loaf tin with butter.

Put the butter, sugar and golden syrup into a pan and heat gently, stirring, until melted. Add the milk, pour into a jug and leave to cool for a couple of minutes, then add the egg.

Sift the flour, ginger, cinnamon and bicarbonate of soda into a large bowl. Pour in the wet ingredients and gently mix together. Mix in the raisins.

Pour the cake mixture into the prepared tin and bake for 1 hour (50 minutes for a ring tin) or until a skewer inserted into the centre of the cake comes out clean. Turn onto a wire rack and leave to cool.

Serves 8

100g/3½oz butter, cut into cubes, plus extra for greasing

100g/3½oz dark soft brown sugar

3 tbsp golden syrup

150ml/5fl oz milk

1 large egg

150g/5oz plain flour

2 tsp ground ginger

2 tsp ground cinnamon

1 tsp bicarbonate of soda

75g/3oz raisins

'Everyday one day

Sweet Potato Pudding

Don't fancy the thought of potatoes in your pudding? Well, think carrot cake – it's the same kind of thing. Add sugar and spice and all things nice and no one will ever guess this has got any vegetables in it at all – they'll just be asking you for the recipe.

Preheat the oven to 190°C/375°F/Gas Mark 5 and grease a 30 x 20cm/12 x 8in rectangular tin with butter.

Put the sweet potato, pumpkin, sugar, butter, ginger, vanilla essence, sultanas, raisins, allspice and coconut into a large bowl and mix together, then stir in 250ml/9fl oz water until evenly mixed.

Spoon the mixture into the prepared tin and bake for 1 hour until firm. Cut into squares and serve warm or cold.

Serves 12

50g/2oz butter, melted, plus extra for greasing

1kg/2lb 4oz sweet potato, peeled and grated

250g/9oz pumpkin, peeled and grated

250g/9oz golden caster sugar

1cm/½in piece fresh root ginger, peeled and grated

1 tsp vanilla essence

50g/2oz sultanas

50g/2oz raisins

1 tsp ground allspice (pimento)

1 coconut, 'meat' grated or 250g/9oz desiccated coconut

bucket go a well
de battam will drop out'

You need to give back what you take

Jamaican Coffee and Rum

As I'm a Rasta man, I won't be drinking the rum, but Jamaican coffee and rum are famous, so here's my Roots recommendation for a Caribbean take on an Irish coffee.

Put the fresh coffee into a jug or cafetière and pour on the boiling water. Leave to brew for a few minutes.

Pour the coffee into 4 glasses, add the sugar, stir to dissolve, then pour in the rum.

Carefully pour on the double cream over the back of a teaspoon so that it floats on top of the coffee.

Serves 4

4 tbsp blue mountain Jamaican fresh ground coffee

4 tbsp soft brown sugar

100ml/3½fl oz dark rum

4 tbsp double cream

'When de rum is in de wit is out'

Don't expect any sense from a drunk person

MY LIFE WITH THE DRAGONS

Since going on Dragons' Den, life has been crazy. Within three weeks of the show, Peter Jones had found me a factory in Wales that could make as much Reggae Reggae Sauce as we needed. He'd also told me he could introduce me to the right man in retail, and he did – Justin King, the chief of Sainsbury's! Peter Jones was instrumental in getting my product on the shelves. From the moment we met on the TV set there was a connection between us.

Sainsbury's placed an initial order for 150,000 bottles of Reggae Reggae Sauce. They thought it would last all year, but everybody went mad for the sauce after Dragons' Den and they sold out in three days. Now it is in all their big stores and I'm developing new flavours all the time trying to extend the Reggae Reggae brand. Peter Jones has become much more than an investor in my family's business, he is my mentor and it's an honour to call him a friend... yeh. Peter Jones – yu' run tings.

Going back to Notting Hill Carnival was also fantastic. I got welcomed like a returning hero and it meant so much to me because it was like a vindication, the fulfilment of everything I had worked so hard at for so many years. Everybody wanted to clap me on the back and tell me they were proud of me and pleased I had become a success.

Reggae Reggae Sauce has changed my life. I don't think of myself as a celebrity exactly, but I can't easily take the tube or bus anymore because I get everywhere late; people want to talk to me, or take a picture, or ask me to sing the song! It never bothers me: it seems to make them feel good, and that makes me feel good.

My mission now is to promote Caribbean food and make it as popular in Britain as Indian food is. We West Indians have a strong affinity with Britain and the food is great, so it's a match made in Heaven.

I'm also trying to give back to the community and where I came from. I've opened my first takeaway, Papine Jerk Centre, on the Winstanley Estate in Battersea, south London, because I came from the ghetto and I want to feed my people first. They supported me and I wanted to give them something in return. I also do a lot of public speaking, and try to help people feel inspired to follow their own dreams. They can come true!

These are exciting times for me. I'm planning to open a restaurant at the Olympic Village in Stratford and eventually I would like a franchise of Reggae Reggae Caribbean restaurants up and down the land. Plus I'll have a chain of Papine takeaways: that's for my children, their business for them to run.

I'm so proud that I have all my children around me and they are a big part of my success. Zaion and Sharlene both work in the restaurant, and Sharlene was in the video for the Reggae Reggae Sauce song. Bernice is an accountant now and looks after my books. My other kids are all musicians – so they all take after me in one way or another!

My life nowadays is totally unrecognisable from when I was a young boy, running free and happy in Jamaica. It's been an incredible story but I feel like it's only just starting. There are a lot more turns and twists to come yet, and I'm looking forward to them.

I recently got an award from the Jamaican High Commission and it turned out that the High Commissioner is from my little Jamaican village of Content! I was in his office for hours, reminiscing fondly about the village and the people there, and I will never forget that a little paradise called Content – and my saintly grandmother, Miriam Small, helped to make me the success I am now.

I hope you have enjoyed my life story, and I hope even more that you enjoy making my recipes and getting to understand Caribbean cooking. Enjoy it – and never forget to put some music in your food!

One love.

Levi Roots

RESOURCES

You'll be surprised by how many Caribbean ingredients are now available from larger supermarkets; otherwise you can find a wealth of exciting ingredients from specialist stores, street markets and websites.

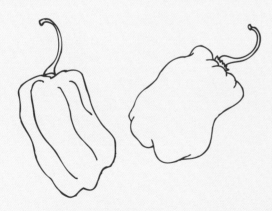

Afro Mini Market
29 Electric Avenue
Brixton
London SW9
020 7274 8819

The Asian Cookshop
28 Fairfield Road
Braintree
Essex
CM7 3HF
01376 349009

Beautiful Foods Ltd
Unit 10c, Lewisham Business Centre
Juno Way Industrial Estate,
London SE14 5RW
020 8469 4117

Calabash Foods
110 Cricklewood Broadway
Cricklewood
London NW2
020 8208 1542

Caribbean Market
27 Chatsworth Road,
London,
E5 0LH
020 8985 9381

D&D Tropical Food Shop,
4 Station Road
Walthamstow,
London E17
020 8503 7693

Esme's
Organic Fruits, Vegetables and Foods
16A Market Row
Brixton London
SW9 8LD

Eunice Tropical Food Shop
133A Deptford High Street
Deptford
London SE8 4NR
020 8469 3095

Sana Food Store
10-12 Granville Arcade
Brixton
London SW9 8PR
020 7274 0005

Websites:
www.caribfoods.co.uk
www.malikstores.co.uk (also a retail
outlet)

Malik Online
24 Stapleton Road
Bristol BS5 0QX
0117 955 1741
www.afrocaribbeanfood.co.uk

CARIBBEAN MARKETS

Brixton Market
Europe's biggest Caribbean food market. The open air market depends on the weather, but generally the market is open Mon-Sat from 10am to sunset.

Shepherd's Bush Market
Buzzy traditional street market offering ethnic food from around the world.
Mon-Sat from 9am to 6pm, early close on Thursday

Ridley Road Market, Hackney
International foods, music and clothes. Open 6am to 6pm.

CARIBBEAN COMMUNITY

www.itzcaribbean.com
The online resource for the Caribbean community and Caribbean culture in the UK. Packed full of information relating to all things Caribbean in London and around the UK.

Finally, don't forget to log onto my sites for free downloads, recipes and reggae updates, www.cookwithlevi.com and www.reggae-reggae.co.uk.

INDEX

ACKNOWLEDGEMENTS

The publishers would like to thank the following for permission to reproduce their images in this book:

p24 (top) Sally and Richard Greenhill/Alamy Stock Photo; p24 (bottom) © Paul Souders; pp25, 30, 34–35, 77, 140, 141 (bottom) Levi Roots; p29 © Fridmar Damm; p31 Jenny Matthews/Alamy Stock Photo; pp40–41 jlvphoto/Getty Images; p54 (inset) Rainer Hackenberg/Getty Images; pp54–55 (main) Eye Ubiquitous/Robert Harding; pp54–55 (bottom), Topcris/Alamy Stock Photo; p61 Paul Souders/Getty Images; pp76–77 (main) Hemis/Alamy Stock Photo; p81 Janine Wiedel Photolibrary/Alamy Stock Photo; p82 VStock/Alamy Stock Photo; pp86–87 Angelo Cavalli/Getty Images; pp90–91 Noel Powell/Shutterstock; pp96–97 Nik Wheeler/Corbis via Getty Images; p113 © Jeremy Horner; pp114–115 Jon Arnold Images/Alamy Stock Photo; p114 (bottom) Terry Harris Just Greece Photo Library/Alamy Stock Photo; p115 (top) Marina Spironetti/Alamy Stock Photo; p115 (bottom) Kendra Nielsen/Shutterstock; p120 Jenny Matthews/Alamy Stock Photo; p121 Photobyte/Alamy Stock Photo; pp122–123 Chris George/Alamy Stock Photo; p141 (top) Eye Ubiquitous/Superstock; p147 WorldFoto/Alamy Stock Photo; p174 Dave G Houser/Getty Images; p177 (inset) Nick Hanna/Alamy Stock Photo